Human

Animal
Series editor: Jonathan Burt

Human

Amanda Rees and Charlotte Sleigh

REAKTION BOOKS

*For John Forrester, whose benign ghost haunted our discussions,
and who remains incontestably human*

Published by
REAKTION BOOKS LTD
Unit 32, Waterside
44–48 Wharf Road
London N1 7UX, UK
www.reaktionbooks.co.uk

First published 2020
Copyright © Amanda Rees and Charlotte Sleigh 2020

Printed and bound in India by Replika Press Pvt. Ltd

A catalogue record for this book is available from the British Library

ISBN 978 1 78914 214 3

Contents

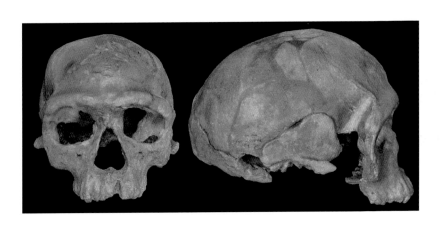

Introduction:
Homo sapiens

The only known surviving species in its genus, *Homo sapiens* is nonetheless categorized as of 'Least Concern' by the International Union for the Conservation of Nature's Red List of threatened or endangered species. As the authors of the list point out, 'the species is very widely distributed, adaptable, currently increasing, and there are no major threats resulting in an overall population decline', although 'some subpopulations may be experiencing localized declines as a result of disease, drought, war, natural disasters and other factors'. *Homo sapiens*, the list notes, has 'the widest distribution of any terrestrial mammal species, inhabiting every continent'. Indeed, its distribution goes beyond even the bounds of Earth: 'a small group of humans has been introduced to space, where they inhabit the International Space Station', and plans are afoot to colonize Mars.[1] Perhaps it is not surprising then that the exploration of strange new worlds has been central to both the history of the human species and to our scientific understandings of the species' origins. Having appeared somewhere in East Africa, sometime before 200,000 years ago, anatomically modern human beings soon found themselves with itchy feet, and set off on their global journey.

Or did they? The dates, places and names associated with human origins and evolution have all been, and still are, subject to vehement, and sometimes violent, controversy. Darwin might,

Casts of the Jebel Irhoud (Morocco) skulls, one of the earliest known examples of *Homo sapiens* fossils.

when writing *On the Origin of Species*, have refrained from commenting on human evolution, but his reticence was swiftly replaced by vigorous debate. In the same year that *Origin* was published, in 1859, scientific recognition of fossilized, apishly human remains did nothing to settle the quandaries surrounding human ancestry. If anything, these concerns intensified over the course of the next century as the precise relationship between apes and other hominins, both extant and extinct, was questioned and contested. In fact, so many different versions of these relationships emerged that by 1934 the anatomist Sir Arthur Keith was able to write an entire book – *The Construction of Man's Family Tree* – on the different interpretations of the fossil record made by Ernst Haeckel, Henry Fairfield Osborn, Eugène Dubois, Grafton Elliot Smith and many other scientists.[2]

By the 1950s it was becoming possible to attach specific dates to the human origin story. The development of more accurate methods of measuring the age of a fossil (fluorine absorption dating, radiocarbon dating) resulted in the serious pruning of many of these family trees. Fossils supposedly ancient were revealed as disappointingly modern, an§d had to be excised from the human genealogy. The relationships between those which remained had to be rethought – were they distant great-great-grandparents to *Homo sapiens*, or just fourth or fifth cousins, many times removed? The idea that there were a number of different places of human origin, since different races had emerged and evolved independently – known as polycentrism, or polygenism – still circulated at mid-century, popularized by individuals such as Franz Weidenreich and Carleton Coon. Importantly, these theories should not be confused with multiregionalist approaches to human evolution, not least because Coon used these ideas to argue for Caucasian racial superiority (and is now disregarded by modern anthropologists). It is equally important to note, however, that assumptions about race – and gender – have long roots in the history of efforts to understand the human species.

Multiregionalism emerged in the 1980s, with the work of the palaeoanthropologist Milford Wolpoff and colleagues, and took a more nuanced approach to the role of place in human evolution.[3] It argued that anatomically modern human beings emerged as the result of a series of evolutionary adaptations that – while having occurred in specific, and different, places – were sufficiently advantageous to spread species-wide. Humanity thus remained a single species, albeit one made up of geographically distinct sub-groups with long evolutionary histories of their own. This approach was directly challenged by the 'Out of Africa' hypothesis. Based on the application of the 'molecular' or 'mitochondrial' clock to the timing of human evolution, fans of this perspective asserted that humanity emerged in one place – Africa – and did so relatively recently, around 200,000 years ago. This theory has powerful evidence in its favour. If we trace the DNA, not of cell nuclei but of mitochondria (passed from mother to child without male intermixing), we find a common ancestor to all living women – a so-called 'Mitochondrial Eve' – who must have lived around this time. Moreover, the earliest known fossils of anatomically modern human beings are dated to this period.[4] In one version or another – since many aspects of the scientific study of human origins remain open to interpretation – the Out of Africa hypothesis remains the scientific model that currently dominates present-day understandings of human evolutionary origins.

But if there is one point on which the scientific community has largely reached consensus, it is that, having once evolved in Africa, members of the genus *Homo* very soon started travelling. At least two waves of migrants, probably driven by drought and climate change, left the continent either via North Africa or by crossing

The 'Willendorf Venus' (carved around 30,000 BCE) is a female figure with no face, but with prominent breasts and buttocks, initially interpreted as a fertility or mother goddess. Recent work by Catherine McCoid and LeRoy McDermott has suggested that it may instead be a female self-portrait, created with the artist looking down at her body.

the Bab-el-Mandeb Strait. Somewhere around 130,000–115,000 years ago, and then again around 700,000 years ago – although these timings are subject to debate – these groups travelled along the coasts of the Arabian peninsula and through Eurasia. The earliest travellers – sometimes referred to as 'archaic humans' – seemed the least successful: that is, they disappear from the fossil record. But in the second wave, humanity went global. From that initial Red Sea crossing, humans spread out to populate Asia. By 65,000 years ago they had reached Australia.[5] By around 40,000 years ago 'moderns' had arrived in Europe, and at the peak of the last Ice Age – around 20,000 years ago – they were probably on Beringia, the land bridge between Siberia and Alaska, although in neither case is it clear how many different groups arrived, nor how large they were.[6] But by perhaps around 18,000 years ago, modern humans had reached South America. Although still comparatively small in absolute numbers, the human species now had a planetary distribution.

Most humans are characterized by bilateral symmetry, possessing two arms, two legs, two eyes, two ears, two nostrils, two nipples and so on. In common with most other great apes, they have no external tails, but do possess an appendix, the purpose of which remains unclear. In fact, the biological similarities between humans, bonobos and chimpanzees are such that scholars have wondered whether a visiting xenobiologist (a biologist of extra-terrestrial life) would classify all three within the same genus (*Pan sapiens*? Or *Homo troglodytes*?).[7] There remain, however, key differences. Unlike the other great apes, humans are extremely good long-distance runners, they excel at throwing things, and have only 23, as opposed to 24, pairs of chromosomes. They are willing to have sex regardless of the reproductive status of their partner. In fact, human females are unique among great apes in that they show no external signals of ovulation. With remarkable

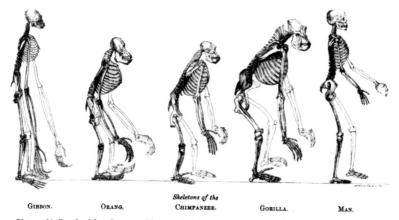

GIBBON.   ORANG.   *Skeletons of the* CHIMPANZEE.   GORILLA.   MAN.

Photographically reduced from Diagrams of the natural size (except that of the Gibbon, which was twice as large as nature), drawn by Mr. Waterhouse Hawkins from specimens in the Museum of the Royal College of Surgeons.

hand–eye coordination, and eyes that respond to electromagnetic radiation in the range of 380 to 740 nm (nanometres), humans use sight, rather than hearing or smell, as their primary sense. While they might appear considerably less hairy than other apes, they actually possess many more hair follicles than chimpanzees. *Sapiens* males tend to be larger and stronger than females, and to speak in a deeper voice, while females tend to have more body fat and to live longer – but overall, humans show far less sexual dimorphism than do the other great apes. In fact, there is often more physical and biological variation within, rather than between, the sexes. Depending on location and heritage, the appearance of *Homo sapiens* individuals can differ dramatically in size and shape, hair and eye colour, and skin colour and texture – to the extent that, as noted, some scholars wondered whether these might reflect different points of evolutionary origin.

However, in general, all members of the human species share certain key anatomical adaptations – and of the suite of physical

Thomas Huxley's 1863 comparison of human and ape skeletons demonstrated the anatomical similarities between the different species, and was intended to demonstrate that they had evolved from a common ancestor.

Stencilled outlines of human hands at the Cueva de las Manos (Cave of the Hands), Santa Cruz, Argentina. Opposable thumbs (together with the capacity for close hand–eye coordination) have often been considered to be a unique human characteristic.

characteristics that have historically been tagged as 'human universals', three stand out as the most frequently cited, particularly when attempting to distinguish between 'humans' and other apes. These characteristics are bipedalism, a large brain (relative to body size) and a remarkably extended period of juvenile dependency. All three are interrelated and are vital for our understanding of how human societies developed. For example, the relatively narrow pelvis produced by bipedalism makes it much harder – and much more dangerous – for females to give birth to a large-brained baby. As a result, unlike other apes, human females usually need help to give birth – and in a trade-off between the size of the infant head and the width of the maternal pelvis, infants are born in an earlier, much less developed state than are those of other apes, thus leading to the extensive period of dependency. While primates in general produce infants who require a lot of parental care, humans exhibit this characteristic to a marked degree, bearing helpless young who will not achieve independence for many years. Women who can draw on reliable and strong social networks and alliances – whether based on

Virgin and the Child, St Catherine's Monastery, Egypt, c. 6th century CE. The iconic central image of mother and child, reflective of humans' extended juvenile dependency, has played a key role in several major world religions.

kinship, legal contracts or mutual attraction – are much more likely to rear these infants to adulthood. It is no accident that humans are the most sociable and the most cooperative of all the apes.

The particular shapes that these networks take can be even more varied than the human beings who populate them. The complex of biological characters that, taken together, tend to characterize the human species – extended dependency, language, tool-use, the menopause (a phenomenon rarely seen in other mammal species) – created the conditions in which humans have developed incredibly complex cultures, with tremendous variation across time and space.[8] These traditions have themselves had a major impact on the ways in which human biology (life expectancy, diet, exhibition of sexual dimorphism and movement through developmental phases) expresses itself, to the point where

Killer whales are one of only two other mammal species where females are known to go through the menopause, enabling 'grandmothers' to play a role in nurturing their grandchildren.

'nature' cannot meaningfully be disentangled from 'nurture'. They have also meant, as this book will show, that people of one particular culture can sometimes find it hard to recognize the common humanity they share with members of another cultural tradition.

Diet is a wonderful example of this. *Homo sapiens* is a generalist omnivore – fully capable of eating and surviving on a diet that derives from both animals and plants, including fungi and algae. But humans consistently and actively reject the edibility of much of what they could eat. What they consider food is entirely dependent on the expectations of their culture. Anthropologists and sociologists have found that food taboos are some of the strongest and most viscerally held beliefs that people can possess: regardless of its edibility, the very idea of eating something forbidden can literally sicken someone. Almost all of the major religions followed by present-day human populations either currently, or have in the past, operated food taboos of one sort or another. Other factors influencing the 'edibility' of food include whether it has been cooked, the soil in which it is grown and the conditions under which animals are harvested or slaughtered. For almost all modern societies (leaving aside the role played by the body and blood of Christ in Christian communion), the most heavily tabooed 'food' of all is human flesh. Whether done in desperation, insanity, perversity or reverence, those who turn cannibal are usually treated as monstrous, as if they have lost their humanity: it is no accident that this accusation is most frequently deployed as a weapon when communities are at war with each other. It's much easier to kill an enemy that isn't human.

Around 12,000 years ago, the Neolithic Revolution took place – a bio-cultural transformation in which *Homo sapiens* transitioned from hunting and gathering to settled agriculture, marked by the emergence of larger centres of population and evidence of

Peter Paul Rubens,
*Saturn Devouring
his Son*, 1636,
oil on canvas.
In classical
mythology,
Cronos, the
father of Zeus,
ate his children
as they were born,
in fear that they
would grow up
to dethrone him.
No act could be
more inhumane.

domesticated animals and plants. Like every other species, humans had existed as part of a complex ecological web – now, human activities, while still constrained by their local environment, began to make deliberate changes within it. Other plants and animals – whether horses, pigs or potatoes – were changed beyond recognition through their encounters with human societies: at the same time, humans and humanity were themselves transformed by and through these relationships. One example of this is directly related to diet – specifically, the capacity to digest milk, which emerged around 7,500 years ago, somewhere in central Europe, and is now widely, although by no means universally, dispersed among the global population.[9]

Like choice of diet, buildings and bodily coverings are an expression of something more than just physiological need; they are another physical demonstration of belonging to a particular culture. Clothing, for example, depends on social context as much as environmental context, changing (like diet) according to season, economic position, national and local traditions and the stage

Kalesh women in traditional dress.

of life cycle. Key differences in individual status and background can be signalled by the location and extent of skin exposed by clothing; its colour and cut; the degree to which that cut follows the outline of the torso, limbs or head; the amount and type of ornamentation; and its capacity to exaggerate elements of human anatomy. Frequently, the mild level of sexual dimorphism exhibited by humans is exaggerated by the choice of clothing, as certain physical areas are padded while others are constricted so as either to appear or become smaller. National dress, from kilt to kimono, is still worn – even if only rarely – to mark membership of a particular ethnic tradition, while the right to wear other items, such as war bonnets or saris, is tensely contested. Body modification – in the form of piercings, ringings, tattoos, branding, implants, excisions and other forms of surgery – is also often undertaken, whether voluntarily or involuntarily, in order to signal membership within, or rejection of, a particular group.

In fact, the one constant in the stunning diversity of human culture is the extent to which these differences are used to distinguish between who is fully human, and who is not. Those who conform to expectations of appearance and demeanour can be acknowledged as persons. Those who do not, are not. Neither category is determined by biology, and 'humanity' is not synonymous with 'personhood'. Human beings can be, and often are, treated as less than human: at the same time, certain categories of non-human animals can become people. Companion animals, for example, might belong to a different species, but can nevertheless become family members. They participate in the celebration of birthdays, holidays and other festivals – and when they die, they are mourned.[10] In contrast, humans who are not recognized as 'people' can very easily become not-human – they are cockroaches, vermin; they infest cities and swarm over borders. They are savages, invaders or monsters. Those who do not behave in a 'civilized' way – that is, in a way that is recognized by the prevailing culture as appropriate – are brutes.[11]

Across time and space, enquiring into humanity has tended to mean establishing, consciously or not, what is *not* human. It slides into, or rather grows out of, a tendency to downgrade the status of other members of *sapiens* as non-human, and means that these less-than-human humans are stripped of their societal status as persons. Depending on one's place in the world, one might ask, why is a Rohingya not a human? Why is a chimp not a human? Why is a robot not a human? The first of these questions is deeply offensive; the second may give pause for thought; and the third

A dog's grave at the Portmeirion Pet Cemetery in Wales marks the burial of a non-human person.

Art and literature have often comically reversed human and animal roles in order to question what it is to be human, as in this cartoon of foxes from the *Illustrated London News* (December 1902).

is perhaps a diverting philosophical conundrum. Nevertheless, they are all statements of the same kind: 'what kind of x are humans such that we may exclude y?' As we enquire further into some of these types of statement, we find that even apparently innocuous non-human categories, such as the automaton, are deployed to manufacture the categories of human and non-human *within* the species *Homo sapiens*.[12] (Some people are just, no offence, a bit mechanical, don't you find?) Numerous groups have tried to define humanity, but whether their authority rests on scientific, theological or legal claims to universality, it's plain that the human has not so much been created in God's image as it has mirrored that of powerful individuals within its various cultures. Non-human categories are used as typologies to explain why those without power tend also to be defined as less than human.

All this has made it rather difficult to write a *Human* book for the Animal series. We cannot show how 'humans' have been portrayed in art, music, myth, economics, medicine, history and politics, in the way that the badger, or the lion, or the shark or the flamingo could be revealed. If we tried, we would only produce another set of culturally specific stories, reflecting prejudices of which we, as authors, are unaware, but that would, undoubtedly, be painfully obvious to the reader. Instead, we have chosen to take a different approach. We will explore how acts of human definition have always emerged out of negotiation, and have reflected the social structures of given societies. Deeply aware of our own position as products of a particular time and place, we will examine the different categories against which powerful

Dehumanizing antisemitic Nazi propaganda, from *Der Stumer*, September, 1944, showing a monstrous insect crawling over the world.

individuals, groups and institutions have measured themselves and (usually) come off best. We will show how the categories of beast, hominin, machine, female, god and alien have operated in the myths, art, histories, sciences, technologies and theologies of human cultures, shifting the limits and liminality of the human according to social, political and economic need.

Humanity, we suggest, is something that *cannot* be defined, and perhaps should not even be thought of as species-bound. Instead, it is the *act* of inclusion – not the content of what, or who, is included – that frames humanity. Humanity, if it exists at all, can never be claimed or conferred but exists in the fragile, fleeting act of conferral: in the realization of relationship with the Other. We return to this topic in the conclusion, under the name of 'imhumanism'.

1 Beast

What distinguishes humans from animals is . . . Although there might be some debate about how exactly this sentence should be finished, there has been – in Western cultures – very little debate about its premise. At least, such was the case until recently. The writer Douglas Adams gave voice to the rising suspicion that things were not so clear-cut:

> on the planet Earth, man had always assumed that he was more intelligent than dolphins because he had achieved so much – the wheel, New York, wars and so on – whilst all the dolphins had ever done was muck about in the water having a good time. But conversely, the dolphins had always believed that they were far more intelligent than man – for precisely the same reasons.[1]

Adams perfectly skewers the hubris of humans' presumed supremacy. His method of doing so, perhaps surprisingly, is Aristotelian. Aristotle was deeply interested in the animal kingdom, but unlike his teacher Plato, he did not organize its inhabitants into a hierarchical taxonomy (wherein, for example, a cat might be an inferior sort of lion). Instead, Aristotle, in his philosophy, has each creature fulfil its own nature: a cat has cat-ness, a lion, lion-ness. Once we admit humans to such a natural history, there are no possible grounds to measure them against another kind.

Between and beyond Aristotle and Adams, however, a host of thinkers have proposed differences that sharply delineate humans and all other kinds of animal. In both traditional and modern Chinese idiom, the less-than-human person who does not act upon his or her Confucian goodwill (ren, 仁) is very frequently slurred with an animal epithet. The possession of a soul is the classic Christian definition of a human being, even though the religion's roots in Judaism and Greek philosophy make this a hard distinction to maintain. *Anima*, the soul, relates to everything that

This terracotta vase, *c.* 520–510 BCE, shows armed soldiers riding dolphins. It can either represent the human mastering the beast, or a collaboration between them that culminated in the imagined act of transportation by dolphins.

is animate – that is, animals too; and in Judaic theology, the *ruach* (חוּר), or the spirit of God, is also the breath of animals. The medieval philosopher Thomas Aquinas got around the problem by positing a hierarchy of souls – vegetative, animal and rational. Humans, for Aquinas, have some of the animal soul – also known as the sensitive soul – because they use their senses in the same way as animals to navigate their way around the world. However, their immaterial, intellectual qualities of mind are evidence of a non-material thing that pervades the body – a true soul. Some Daoist teaching, too, suggests that something special (translated as 'understanding') generally exists in humans, but qualifies that it is not necessarily a property of their physical form; a human may have the mind of a 'brute', while according to certain ancient sages, 'there [is] no wide gulf [in mind and understanding] between any of the living species endowed with blood and breath.'[2]

Writing in the seventeenth century, the philosopher John Locke broadly accepted Aquinas' distinction, but placed the stress upon rationality for its own sake, rather than using it as proxy for a soul.[3] Like Aristotle, he posited that 'animal spirits' conduct information about sight, sound and touch to our minds; but it seemed to him that even with their powers of learning and simple reasoning, animals were not capable of making comparisons or forming generalities or abstractions. Yet even with this distinction in place, Locke rejected the common definition of humans as 'rational animals'. To persuade his readers, he invited them to consider how they would feel if they saw something that looked like a human, but 'had no more reason . . . than a cat or a parrot'. This creature, he surmised, readers 'would call . . . still a man'. Contrary-wise, if readers should 'hear a cat or a parrot discourse, reason, and philosophize', he was pretty sure they would 'think it nothing but a cat or a parrot', albeit 'a very intelligent and rational one'.

Pigsy is a half-human, half-pig monster from the classic 16th-century Chinese novel *Journey to the West*. In this image, Pigsy succumbs to earthly temptations by accepting food, while Xuanzang, unmoved, and Monkey look on.

At this point in his essay, Locke tells a story that he had heard concerning a parrot in Brazil, from a witness who was himself sceptical. The witness reported the following dialogue (the human's voice in roman, and the parrot's in italics):

Where do you come from?
From Marinnan.
. . . What do you do there?
I look after the chickens.
[Laughing] You look after the chickens?
*Yes, me; and I know how to do it well [makes chucking noise
that is used to call them]*

Locke is in evident discomfort about this story; he waves it away
as something for the naturalists to think about, and yet he feels
compelled to tell it. He goes to some lengths to credit the piety
and honesty of the witness (at least, as he tells us, he 'passed for
a very honest and pious man').

Over the past few decades parrots have been a prime candidate
for rupturing the supposition of human uniqueness. Language
is supposed to be special to *Homo sapiens* – and yet parrots can
talk, can't they? Alex (1976–2007), an African grey parrot, was
trained by scientist Irene Pepperberg, apparently demonstrating
an ability not only to mimic, but to form precisely the kind of
generalizations that Locke thought were out of reach to animals.
He learned more than one hundred words, but, more significant
than that, he also learned to deploy concepts to perform simple
arithmetic, to coin new words of his own and to manipulate categories such as bigger/smaller, some/none or same/different.[4]

The traditional European model of animal cognition is captured by the term 'sagacity', a very particular and instinctual form
of wisdom that in some ways brought animals close to unfallen,
divine knowledge. In the biblical Book of Numbers, it is Balaam's
ass, and not the prophet, his owner, who is able to see the angel
of the Lord. The first definition of the word 'sagacity' in the *Oxford
English Dictionary* is given not as wisdom, but as acuity in the
sense of smell. In 1607 Edward Topsell referred to 'sagacity or

Glottifmi modulationum fibilo exprimendi in Lufcinia obferuati

Pigolifmus

Glazifmus Teretifmus Pigolifmus

Teretifmus Glazifmus

Pigolifmus Glazifmus Chromatico–enharmonicum nefcio

quid affectans Pigolifmus Glazifmus

Pigolifmus Pigolifmus Glazifmus Teretifmus

Diuerfarum uolucrium voces
notis muficis exprefiæ

Vox parturientis Gallinæ

to to toto to toto to ✳ to toto to toto to toto ✳

Gallicinium

Cuculcu Cuculci Cuculcu

A

B

Gallina conuocans pullos

glo glo glo

C

Vox Cuculi

Gucu gucu gucu ✳ gucu

E

Vox Coturnicis

Bikebik bikebik bikebik

D

Κοϊσε

Parrots have long been companion animals of humans, remarkable for their ability to acquire, or at least mimic, human language.

smell in dogs'; other quotations of sample use refer to animals and birds and that other less-than-human species, 'Ladies'. Sagacity, then, describes both the highest wisdom of humans and the sniffing know-how of dogs. Because it applies to both it implies gentle criticism of human psychological hubris as well as an enjoyable sense of excitement and pleasure at what animals are able to do. Even when used for humans (that is, men) in the sense of wisdom and mental acuity, the word gestures at its own limits. It is often used in a negative context, to describe a wisdom that is missing, or to denote preternatural wisdom beyond ordinary human capacities. An ability to predict the future is preeminent among these; one of the most culturally pervasive instances of animal sagacity

Rather than interpreting the sounds of animals as language alone, Athanasius Kircher's *Musurgia universalis* (1650) presents the sounds animals make as music. By doing so, Kircher's work asks us to seek not only rationality, but beauty within the sounds of animals.

is their supposed ability to predict earthquakes and tsunamis. Travellers' narratives from the eighteenth and nineteenth centuries were packed with believe-it-or-not tales of animal sagacity, often provocatively counterpoised against human achievements. A favourite example concerned the abilities of ants to construct bridges, or avoid death by crushing on railway tracks – and all without the mental capacities of Victorian engineers. The trope of animal sagacity remains with us in the twenty-first century, with many reports of animal avoidance of the Asian tsunami of December 2004. Such reports have provoked continued experiment and at least one patent application for disaster prediction. Yet the whole area of alternative animal cognition remains tainted with an air of medieval hokum. This leaves animal cognition in a scientific no man's land. If it is not like our mode of thinking, animal cognition cannot be explored by science; and if it is like ours, then it is scientifically unprovable and/or most likely absent.

Other famous linguistic experiments have been performed on species much closer to humankind than parrots: species that may, perhaps, be permitted something approaching human cognition. Various chimps and gorillas have been taught words using American Sign Language. Unsurprisingly, these accomplishments – like Alex's – have been controversial, attracting allegations of fraud or at the very least self-delusion on the part of experimenters; the apes, it is claimed, are engaging in imitation or have learned to please their trainers without an understanding of what they are doing. Some apes have been taught language in socially sterile lab conditions, while others have been immersed in rich social environments with their human keepers and their families. The latter type of experiment, including Alex's, is more strongly associated with success in language acquisition, and for this very reason is also less replicable and hence regarded as less 'scientific'.

Science has no place for the relationship-embedded language that emerges from these exchanges, these cat's cradles of human–animal knowledge so delicately held between one set of hands and another set of paws or claws.

The semiotician Thomas Sebeok had a different way of cutting the Gordian knot of cognition, language and humanity. To him, the question of language was the wrong starting point; the underlying matter was communication. Biological life *was* a matter of communication: a functional system of information exchange and feedback. A linguistic or conscious grasp of that system was neither here nor there: a subset at best. To think about communication without language, one need look no further than the ants, which communicate complex needs, demands and interrogations with chemical molecules.[5] Thus communication is extended to animals, but at the expense, potentially, of admitting that human language, or much of it, is not as special as we like to think. 'Nice weather'; 'vote for change'; so many of our utterances have a functional role in maintaining social arrangements but are phatic and empty of meaningful content – bringing us closer to Sebeok's animals.

The directive logic of Sebeok's theory, closing the gap between animals and humans, is out of step with Western preferences. In general, scientists and philosophers have worked to retain it. During the latter part of the nineteenth century, scientists engaged in a frantic process of hierarchy-building, placing different races and creatures upon a continuum of progress, from the basic to the highly evolved, and from the savage to the civilized.

Darwin applied a patina of respectability to a range of pre-existing theories about continuity in the natural world, most especially between animals and humans. What had previously been matters of theoretical or developmental priority (that is, which faculties developed first, or should be considered as basic), were now given a history that stretched for aeons, between transmuting species. As Victorian scientists weighed up the likely order of bipedalism, social living, culture, tool use and brain size in the story of animal to human, their emphases inevitably reflected what they thought was most important, if not unique, about themselves. Their Anglocentric accounts culminated in the uncritical acceptance of the Piltdown Man fraud, a crude concoction of a proto-human, comprised of a modern human skull and an orang-utan jaw, and complete with primitive cricket bat as marker of his evolved status.

Alfred Russel Wallace, co-describer of natural selection, differed from Darwin when it came to the human question. Indeed, most writers of the period tended to treat 'primitive' tribes as highlighting qualities still in the process of developing. Wallace, by contrast, held that the educability of so-called savages indicated a kind of spare capacity in their brains that could not be explained by natural selection. (Natural selection cannot, by definition, work on an unexpressed quality.) The human/animal divide remained, at least in his mind, intact.

The decades following Darwin were contradictory in their responses to new perspectives on animal–human relations, in at least two areas. The first of these, chronologically speaking, concerned animal sensation and pain. Evolution's mental continuum suggested that an emotional, sensitive and cognitive relativism was now warranted, of the sort that Darwin himself explored in *The Expression of the Emotions in Man and Animals* (1872). Yet at the very same time, and in the very same circles (notably, Thomas Huxley's), the strongest and most explicit defences of vivisection were made. Meanwhile, the persons who were issuing the loudest calls for 'humane' treatment of animals were dismissed as merely silly (and generally female), victims of a most unscientific subjectivity.

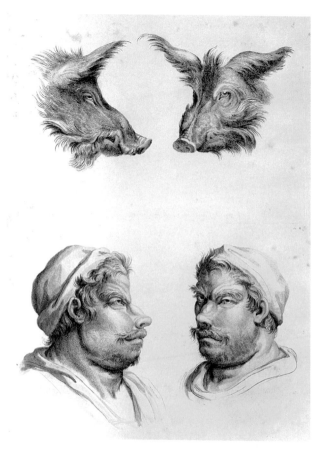

The noted 17th-century portraitist Charles Le Brun was deeply interested in the connections between human and animal physiognomy, as in this image of 1671.

A similar paradox emerged in the early twentieth century. Psychologists – at that time working across human and animal boundaries – began to assert that animal instincts, buried in the evolutionary cellar of the human mind, accounted for a good deal of human action. At the same time, a doctrine was laid down in comparative psychology, known as Morgan's canon, stating that

Leonardo Da Vinci, *Lady with an Ermine*, 1489–90, oil on wood panel. Leonardo's portrait seems to go beyond the conventional symbolism attached to the ermine – purity, pregnancy or a pun on the subject's name – and suggests a genuine intimacy and rapport between human and animal.

no animal behaviour should be interpreted in terms of higher psychological processes if it could be interpreted in terms of processes lower in the scale of psychological evolution. That the canon could have, with good reason, wiped out conscious explanations of human behaviour was not considered: the law maintained the distinction at just the time when science otherwise eroded it. The human/animal boundary demanded protection.

When did apes transform into humans? Where, when and what is the 'missing link' between them? Such evolutionary questions, spawned in the late nineteenth and early twentieth centuries, were catered to in the many circuses and sideshows that featured ape men, bearded women and nondescripts, and were profitably mounted in the U.S. and the UK. In an era in which descriptions of evolutionary mechanisms remained fluid, such persons were proposed as throwbacks to the ancestors of the truly human. Although gentlemen of science were more restrained in their interpretations of such genetically unusual persons – few accepted the mixed orang-human parentage proposed for the much-exhibited 'bearded lady' Julia Pastrana, for example – the same racialized, unhealthy interest in their liminal human status appeared to hold. These shows were, after all, only a special example of the animal transformation stories that had been told for millennia. By turns titillating and perturbing, they were part of a culturally widespread attempt to probe the nature and limits of humanity.

Animal transformation stories often speak, specifically, to the otherwise unspeakable: the sexual mores of the human animal. There has been a major reversal of the mechanism, however, in Western culture. During the Renaissance, painting and sculpture actively exploited classical myths of trans-species sex, creating art that would have been unconscionable with two human subjects.[6] The seduction of Leda by Zeus in the form of a swan was a frequent subject for artists and collectors in Renaissance Italy, often rendered in exquisitely beautiful and erotic form. Sometimes it was all a bit too much; Louis, duke of Orléans (1703–1752), was supposedly so tortured by a Correggio rendering of the subject that he slashed at the figure of Leda with a knife. The painting, restored by another hand, still survives, but many others have been lost, perhaps suffering a similar puritanical fate. The

Poster from the 1850s advertising the supposed human-ape in-betweener, Julia Pastrana.

Renaissance fashion for paintings of Leda was lost to art for around three hundred years.

W. B. Yeats's poem on the myth coincided with a rediscovery of Leda's seduction in nineteenth- and twentieth-century art: 'And how can body, laid in that white rush, / But feel the strange heart beating where it lies?' The body is Leda's, but whose is the heart? The breasts of the two are, as Yeats has already told us, pressed together. The lines come at the crux point of the poem, where Leda's resistance gives way to something like pleasure. The ambiguity is deliberate; Yeats speculates that along with desire, so too knowledge, and power with it, are transferred from one being to the other.

Correggio's *Leda and the Swan*, *c.* 1530, oil on canvas, depicting Jupiter's seduction/ rape of a princess, has been the subject of controversy, physical attack and revisionist restoration. Debate has centred on the degree of chasteness present in Leda's smile.

Some seven or eight decades after Cranach the Elder made this apparently fantastical woodcut of a werewolf in *c.* 1510–15, Peter Stumpp of Epprath, Cologne, was brutally executed for the crime of lycanthropy.

Strange currents, to read this poem and feel its historical undertow oneself. An elderly friend recently confided to one of the authors that her late husband believed Yeats may have been his father, his mother having worked as a young domestic in a house at which the poet was a frequent guest. Placing their photographs side by side, one could believe it. And in addition to physical appearance, the fact that the late husband, too, was a literate and cultured man, a staggering cygnet from his unlikely background, seemed to suggest the connection. Of course, the mother's story was one of utter disgrace – no willing embrace of the feathered seducer for her. Yeats's poem makes for uncomfortable reading in a feminist world, its unquestionable beauty embodied in the language of male violence.

We may never know whether or to what extent Leda and similar myths were a Renaissance celebration of rape, as opposed to a simpler paean to the pleasures of the flesh. Today, though, permission and consent are a central feature of anthro-animal sex. Animals, unlike humans, are free to have sex 'naturally', without guilt or restraint. Such was the root of whites' racist fears of the 'bestial' African male slave as hyper-sexual. However, facultative identification with an animal could yield sexual permission for the white male, too. Wolves – and werewolves and vampires – are perhaps the best-established species for the trope.[7] For Jack London's readers, a dog's ability to recover its inner wolf was indicative of the consoling possibility that the urban, white immigrant might recover an autochthonous soul, even on stolen soil. And although the nature writer and Boy Scout pioneer Ernest Thompson Seton styled himself 'Black Wolf', it was the act of killing a wolf that fulfilled his desires. It was the ultimate consummation of his animal nature, inducting him into the most intimate relationship possible with the animal.

The lone wolf prowls through the night, doing what it will. The alpha male, a closely related trope, suggests that homosocial significance actually predominates over sexuality; beating other males to win the female partner is almost more important than the sex itself. Dark, brooding, dominant: these wolves possess a cluster of characteristics that are close to the seducer of romance fiction, a figure whose actions in the realm of fantasy (but *not* reality) have granted 'permission' to the female reader to acknowledge her sexual desire through the imagined renunciation of consent. Historically women have been even more discouraged than men from acknowledging the desires of their 'animal' nature.

Freud's Wolf Man – Sergei Pankejeff (1886–1979) – was deeply mired in sexual guilt. His sister used to frighten him with a particular storybook illustration of an upright wolf; a little later, he had a memorable nightmare in which he saw six or seven white wolves in a tree, looking at him. In a long and complex analysis, Freud concluded that the dream reflected Pankejeff's earlier witnessing of the 'primal scene' – that is, his parents engaged in a sexual act. The dream was a space in which Pankejeff processed his childish logic; he had desired sexual satisfaction from his father, but upon recalling the primal scene that preceded this desire, he had come to perceive that to do so, he must be 'castrated' like his mother. Unable to accept this 'feminine' outcome, his libido was redirected as a fear of certain animals – the wolf – as well as sadistic tendencies towards them. Freud noted that his subject had worked very hard to end up where he began: his fear of his father was disguised as a wolf disguised as a man. Such are the convolved routes of the unconscious: the fear of the animal disguised as a human disguised as an animal.

Later in his paper, Freud reflects on the significance of the fact that Pankejeff saw his parents in a particular sexual position: his mother on all fours, his father standing behind. Moreover, Freud notes that this is the position most commonly cited by other analysands in their recollection of the primal scene. What should one make of this animal encounter? Freud posits the possibility that at least some of his patients have actually witnessed copulation between animals, and then displaced this observation onto their parents, thus explaining their position from behind. This theory has the advantage of intuitive likelihood, as well as resulting in the child's clearer view of the genitals – a crucial part of Freud's analysis – than that obtained from face-to-face positions. Freud even considers the possibility that what we see at work in the analysand's construction of the primal scene is a pre-human, animal intelligence attempting to make sense of things. Thus he equates the bestial and the sexual. The most animal act is the most sexual, and vice versa. The supposed unique human quality

Sigmund Freud's analysis of the Wolf Man and his dream – depicted here in his own painting – marked a turning point in the patient's psychic development.

of making love face-to-face is both affirmed and denied. Yeats's insistence on the face-to-face position of Leda and the swan now takes on fresh significance. The narrative of his poem contains not only the awakening of Leda to sexual knowledge, but, perhaps, the costly education of the human race, in transitioning from the happy ignorance of the animal realm to a troubled state of consciousness.

Freud's equation of masculinity (that is, the evasion of castration) with heterosexual activity looks, at best, quaint by current moral standards. The homosexual fantasies that the Wolf Man went to such trouble to repress are today, in many parts of the world, perfectly acceptable as realities. And yet animals still function, in that curious anima–human–animal convolution, as a vehicle for sexual permission. The word 'anthro' today, in common parlance, summons up not humans but their semiotic relation, animals. Search for 'anthro' on Google Images, and you will find

Furry conventions are recurring gatherings for members of the furry communities on both international and local levels.

the results dominated by humanized animal drawings, in suggestive poses or with genitals coyly X-ed out. (My particular favourite is a tiger with an impressive six-pack, posing in a sports bra.)

There is a fan culture dedicated to all things anthro, whose members go by the name 'furries'. These humans create and consume animal-transformation fiction; they collect animal knick-knacks; they may wear small animal signifiers, such as a fox's tail or furry ears, or don complete fur suits. Their identities, or 'fursonas', are played out online, and, for the most committed, at furry conventions and meetings. They attract a level of hatred and hilarity out of all proportion to their activities: grotesque virtual world, and latterly, social media viciousness. These attacks are pre-eminently targeted towards the presumed sexual mores of furries. Even the anthro-positive podcasters Panda Pause characterize the pivotal moment in visual anthrotransition narratives as sexual in nature. They call it the 'look-down-the-pants' shot, as though the newly embodied animal is inspecting his (their discussion is confined to male exemplars) passport to sexual liberty.[8] The nature of the attacks made upon furries demonstrates with particular clarity the phenomenon of revealing more about oneself through criticism than about one's supposed target. We project our sexuality onto the animal, and we are discomfited in the extreme when furries reflect it back at us. Why should furries be allowed to mate when and how they like, when most of us police ourselves to prevent such things? The venom and laughter provoked by furries suggest that animals touch on some of the deepest and most uncomfortable questions we have about the relation between selfhood and sexuality. One is reminded of a late nineteenth-century description of Louis d'Orléans' sadistic assault upon his father's painting: '[driving] a knife through the fair flesh which Correggio's brush had endowed'.[9] Why not just take it down and put it in a cupboard, if you really don't like it?

Research by social scientists reveals, in fact, rather touching qualities inherent in furry circles. This includes quite literal touching, in some cases: a non-sexual grooming, or scritching, as it is called. Furries are by majority male, and, in the West, this kind of affectionate touch is not usually permitted for them without the cover of a fursuit. Surveys conducted by Sharon Roberts and others find participants similarly highlighting the support, acceptance and non-judgemental acceptance that they receive from fellow furries:[10] 'Usually, I don't talk to people, but I got here and have fuzzy people I want to hug.'[11] Furries also include a very high proportion of persons of non-binary gender, and of non-heterosexual orientation. Furry fan fiction maps a complex zoological taxonomy onto different sexual identities and preferences, such as the gay male bear. Coming-out narratives are central to furry discourse: coming out as a furry is, for many, a rehearsal of sexual coming-out, whether before or after the event. It is almost as though furries have deliberately chosen a despised animal persona – a sub-human category – as a means of effecting this rehearsal. It may be a way of working through society's past and present rejection and persecution, confronting it in a deliberately chosen and extreme form. The particular historic contingencies of animals add further dimensions to this choice. On the one hand, we have a seventy-year history of anthropomorphized animals from Disney and others, adorable to some and cloying to others. Thanks to studios' marketing of these films to children and families, an attack on animal characters is also an attack on children. On the other hand, a sensibility has been slowly intensifying that condemns the persecution of others for merely being different. Finally, animals of all kinds are increasingly seen as the victims of human cruelty. Put all this together, and the fursona is simultaneously a deliberate sub-human provocation, aiming to render explicit prejudice that is otherwise hidden, and an unassailable position of moral superiority.

During the Renaissance, human–animal sex in art was regarded as an acceptable alternative to human–human; today, things are rather the other way around. Amazon has strict rules to police anthro fan fiction. According to fan-fiction writer Mickey Bamboo, humans may have sex only with transformed beings that retain human characteristics. In other words, the rules of consent have been applied to animals. A human-animal may consent to sex, but an animal cannot. Thus Amazon has solved by fiat the great question that has plagued animal studies for decades: whether, and how, we may consider animals to have agency. The reasons for Amazon's decision are unclear – is it a specific fear of inspiring copy-cat action in the real world; is it a general squeamishness about bestiality; or is it indeed a logical extension of consensual mores in the human realm, rendering the very definition of animal-kind parasitic upon human sexual politics?

At the very moment in which animals have been granted agency via sexual consent, they are at their most anthropomorphic.

2 Hominin

What is a hominin? The word doesn't mean the same as 'hominoid', which is a general term used to refer to all apes, nor 'hominid', a related category used to refer to all great apes, whether living or extinct. Instead, it is a term that refers specifically to humans and their close taxonomic relatives. Currently, this means any creature belonging to the genera *Homo* or *Australopithecus*, although others (*Paranthropus*, for example) are sometimes included. As such, it is a very important term when it comes to managing the distinction (and transformation) between humans and beasts.

At present, *Homo sapiens* is the only living member of this category, although we have many extinct relatives. Often, these are family members that we know by their personal names: Lucy (*Australopithecus afarensis*), Turkana Boy (*Homo ergaster*), the Taung Child (*Australopithecus africanus*), Nutcracker Man (*Paranthropus boisei*), Elvis the Pelvis (*Homo heidelbergensis*), the Hobbit (*Homo floresiensis*), the Handy-Man (*Homo habilis*) and Java Man (*Homo erectus*), among others. Names are, after all, very important when it comes to defining what is, and what is not, human, as the controversy that has dogged the nomenclature of one particular group of hominins demonstrates very clearly. Are Neanderthals – the hominin genetically and chronologically closest to us – to be known as *Homo neanderthalensis* or *Homo sapiens neanderthalensis*? Do they belong to our species, or are they separate? Relationships

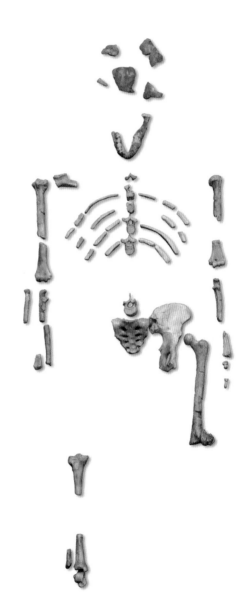

'Lucy', the skeleton
discovered in
1972 in Ethiopia's
Awash Valley by
palaeoanthropologist
Donald Johanson.

between humans and their prehistoric relatives are, to say the least, controversial.

To get a sense of how problematic this issue has been, all you need to do is to take a brief glance at its history. Two hundred years ago, writing a list like the one above would have been unimaginable. In the early nineteenth century, *Homo sapiens* did not have a prehistory. At that time, most Westerners thought that humanity had been specially created in the divine image. There was little or no conceptual space for the notion that human bodies and minds were the product of a long process of evolutionary change over time and place. In fact, the word 'prehistory' itself wasn't used in English until 1836.[1]

But from around the turn of the nineteenth century, scholars were increasingly intrigued by the strangely shaped stones that could sometimes be discovered in quarries or riverbeds – the Hoxne hand-axe from Suffolk, for example, reported by John Frere (an ancestor of renowned palaeoanthropologist Mary Leakey) in 1800, or the artefacts that Boucher de Perthes was uncovering along the banks of the Somme in northern France. Certain caves, such as Goat's Hole on South Wales's Gower Peninsula, or Kent's Cavern in Devon, were known to contain not just flints that looked like tools, but fossils that looked uncannily human. Most disquietingly, they lay alongside bones that seemed monstrous – the petrified remains of animals that no longer walked the Earth.[2]

How old were these artefacts? At first, scholars could only make relative, and deeply subjective, estimates of age by looking at the rock layer where they had been found, and considering any other nearby distinctive remains. Scholars such as Boucher de Perthes were clear on this: where apparently human remains were found in association with the fossils of extinct mammals, this meant that humans must have existed at the same time as these long-dead animals, at a time so long ago as to be nearly beyond imagining.

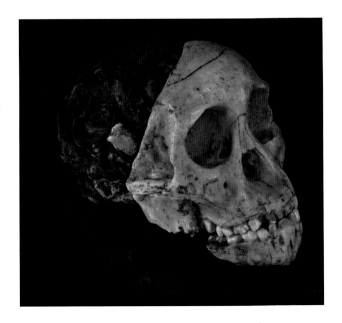

The skull of the 'Taung child', discovered in South Africa, reconstructed by the anatomist Raymond Dart, and now identified as a member of the species *Australopithecus africanus*.

But most early nineteenth-century geologists and antiquarians disagreed vehemently. They argued that rock layers and deposits could easily become confused, either by natural causes or by human activities. Discovering human remains next to extinct animals was coincidental, not evidence for the ancient origins of humanity.

In 1859 this changed. Six months prior to the publication of *On the Origin of Species* – Darwin's reluctant challenge to the divine creation of humanity – an equally world-shattering publication had been sent to the Royal Society of London. In May of that year, the geologist Joseph Prestwich presented an account of the visit he and the archaeologist John Evans had made to the excavations of Boucher de Perthes, at Abbeville on the Somme. There, 'full of doubt', they had inspected the discoveries and had decided that Perthes's interpretation was correct.[3] From this point on, the antiquity of humanity became an increasingly significant subject for scientific investigation – and a key cultural resource for understanding human difference.

It became, for example, quite quickly evident that *Homo sapiens* was not the only kind of human ever to have existed. Strange, but still familiar, skulls and other remains had already been found in the Engis Caves in Belgium (1829); in Forbes' Quarry, Gibraltar; (1848) and – most famously – in the Feldhofer Cave in Germany's Neander Valley (1856). By the end of the century, an entirely unfamiliar – but in some sense hauntingly recognizable – skull was found by Eugène Dubois on the banks of the Solo River in Java (1891). A jaw bone that appeared to fall somewhere in between these two extremes was found near Heidelberg in 1907. Peking Man was identified in the 1920s from discoveries at Zhoukoudian, and in the same decade, Raymond Dart announced the existence of what appeared to be the most ape-like of all specimens so far – his reconstruction of the skull of the Taung Child, found by a group of South African quarrymen.

Some of these finds went on to become type specimens of the hominin species mentioned earlier – but a list of early twentieth-century significant fossils would also have included a number of 'ghost' fossils, bearing different, and now almost forgotten names. Such lists dwelt on Tilbury Man, the Dartford Skull, Galley Hill Man, Grimaldi, Cro-Magnon, Boskop Man, Kanam Man, the Gadarene Skull and – of course – Piltdown Man, complete with his cricket bat.[4] Establishing that now-extinct groups of apparently human beings had existed, and deciding when and how they might have appeared on the human family tree, was not just a process that took a considerable amount of time. It was, and is, a process subject to constant revision, as new discoveries and developments are made and debated by scientists and laypeople alike. Central to these debates were assumptions – sometimes competing and often unstated – of what it meant, and what it means, to be 'human'.

Consistently, what was at stake was the significance of the differences that could be identified between the remains – whether of stone or bone – that were found from the late eighteenth century onwards, and their present-day equivalents. How were these fossils different from the bones of anatomically modern humans? Had these stones been deliberately and consciously shaped, or was their resemblance to the tools of modern hunter-gatherers coincidental? What people were doing here was defining the physical and psychological contours of humanity – how big did the skull need to be before it could house a recognizably human brain? Did large brow-ridges really mean that their possessor wasn't 'human'? What about the shape of the ankle bone? How was the 'sophistication' of a stone hand-axe to be judged, and – in the absence of immediate fossil remains – how was it possible to decide on how old it was, let alone which species might have made or used it?

Underlying all these debates during the late nineteenth and earlier twentieth centuries was the increased contact between imperial Europeans and the peoples of the countries they were in the process of annexing and colonizing. The frequent presumption that local people were less socially and culturally sophisticated than the 'civilizing' Europeans often slid into even less savoury assumptions about relative levels of biological evolution. White (male) Europeans stood at the top of the evolutionary scale constructed according to deeply racist assumptions: hunter-gatherers, in contrast, were primitive, 'Stone-Age' survivals. As a result, discussions about the human status of literal fossils had implications for their metaphorical modern descendants: if one was barely human, surely so was the other?

These unpleasant debates did not just cover whether the bones were human; they raged over the nature of the relationship between their owners and modern humanity. Were these remnants *ancestors* of, or *cousins* to, modern *Homo sapiens*? And what did that imply about their 'humanity'? Remember that in most cases, the physical remains that scientists found were extremely incomplete. The discovery of relatively intact skulls or skeletons was, and is, vanishingly rare. Most announcements were and are based on extrapolations from the meticulous reconstructions of shattered crania or jaws, sometimes only a few teeth, or even – more recently – DNA painstakingly extracted from a single Denisovan finger bone.

Remember, too, that it was not just the anatomy of these individuals that needed to be reconstructed – scholars were also

An image used as part of the frontispiece from Lord Avebury's *Prehistoric Times*, first published in 1865, which (according to its subtitle) used the 'manners and customs of modern savages' to interpret the stones and bones that were being discovered.

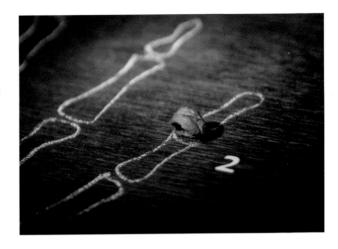

Fragments of bones found in Denisova Cave in 2008 suggest that while Denisovan teeth and jaws might have looked 'primitive', their fingers were just like those of modern humans.

attempting, on the basis of the limited bone-and-stone evidence available, to make predictions with respect to the technology, culture and society of these extinct hominids. Finally, scholars and scientists were not the only people involved and invested in this process: a significant proportion of the general public has been fascinated by human prehistory for at least the last 150 years, and this is a fascination that has been eagerly fed by both scientists and the mass media. In all cases – whether dealing with physical appearance, psychological capacity or social behaviour – researchers were making claims about what was, and was not, to count as human, and these claims were being assessed and evaluated not just by their peers but also by the wider public.

So what can hominins tell us about the different ways in which humanity has been defined, whether in relation to race, species or culture? At the time of writing, there is a tentative consensus that the genus *Homo* contains seven species: one extant, and the others extinct. In the order in which they seem to disappear from the records, these are *rudolfensis* (1.8 million years ago), *habilis*

(1.4 million years ago), *heidelbergensis* (200,000 years ago), *erectus* (143,000 years ago), *floresiensis* (50,000 years ago), *neanderthalensis* (40,000 years ago) and, of course, the still surviving *sapiens*. Two immediate caveats are needed – first, the possible addition of *denisova*, a hominin discovered in 2008, but whose taxonomic status has yet to be resolved, and second, the possible inclusion of both *denisova* and *neanderthalensis* within the category of *Homo sapiens*.[5] Notably, it is Neanderthals – short, stocky, with huge brow-ridges and large noses and, importantly, limited capacity for intelligent speech – that have become synonymous with 'prehistoric' man or 'caveman' in popular culture. In fact, the cultural role played by Neanderthals is at least as important as their scientific position: were they the first Europeans? Were they exterminated by *Homo sapiens* in the first genocide? These questions, together with the fact that it was a Neanderthal fossil that was first to be recognized as a non-human skull, suggests that it is worth examining their case in some detail.

In 1856 quarrymen working in western Germany's Neander Valley unearthed a number of fossilized bones, including part of

Brother and Other? Human (left) and Neanderthal (right) skulls facing each other.

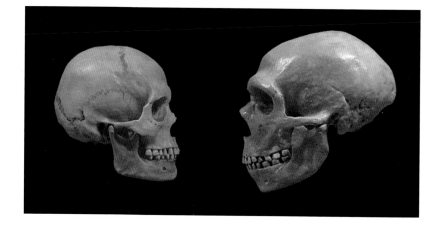

a skull. Hermann Schaaffhausen, professor of anatomy in Bonn, initially identified these as belonging to an individual of a previously unknown race – not species – of humans. England's Thomas Huxley echoed this conclusion, agreeing with Schaaffhausen that while the skull certainly resembled that of an ape as much as it did a human (hence the assumption that it must belong to a member of a non-Caucasian race), the size of the brain case implied an equally large brain – and hence, that its quondam owner must have been human. But in 1863 William King, a professor of geology, took a closer look at the skull. For King, the size of the brain was insufficient when it came to defining the creature as human – the shape had to be considered as well. And in his opinion, the shape was too ape-like to be human: its relative 'flatness' meant that its owner was unlikely to be able to speak, and was, therefore, unlikely to have developed religious or moral feelings. These, for King, were the defining human characteristics. The fossil, therefore, represented a new species (*Homo neanderthalensis*) sharing the same genus with humanity, but remaining distinct and different – not quite human.[6]

The human status of the Neanderthals – not quite brother, often Other – was to shift drastically over the course of the next 150 years. From around 1880 to the outbreak of the First World War, in excavations throughout Europe, from what is now the Czech Republic through Belgium, France, Germany, Croatia and even reaching into Palestine, more and more Neanderthal fossils were found, as individuals and in groups, and even sometimes alongside anatomically modern (but fossil) humans. A whole stone tool industry – the Mousterian culture – was linked with them, so that the presence of characteristic Mousterian axes could be taken as evidence for Neanderthal presence also. Neanderthals might not be humans, but like humans, they could use tools. And points of comparison now existed – although Neanderthal fossils dominated this early period, the identification of Java Man (now *Homo erectus*) in 1895 meant that the Neanderthals were no longer the most primitive human-like fossils known.

But crucially, between 1909 and 1912, two discoveries were made that were to profoundly influence the way in which Neanderthals were treated during the century that followed. In the first place, in 1909, an almost complete Neanderthal skeleton was found in La Chapelle-aux-Saints in France – and in the second, in 1912, fragments of the cranium and jawbone of a new type of hominin were discovered in a gravel pit at Piltdown, in England. The relative completeness of the Old Man of La Chapelle gave scientists their first opportunity to reconstruct Neanderthal anatomy, and in 1911, Marcellin Boule did so. Boule's interpretation showed the Neanderthals as starkly different from humans. Not only were their heads flat, rather than rounded, but their heads jutted forwards from stooped shoulders. Their knees were bent, and they seemed unable to stand fully erect.[7] The contrast with the tall, straight-backed *Homo sapiens* – high-arched head balanced securely atop the spinal column – could not be clearer: Neanderthals were not fully bipedal, and their shambling stance was more reminiscent of ape than human. At the same time, the discovery of Piltdown Man, with its smooth, curving, human-like cranium seemed to emphasize the distance between Neanderthals and the human line of descent, at least so far as English scholars were concerned.

Boule's reconstruction of the 'brutish appearance' of the Neanderthal, and his stress on the likelihood of the 'predominance of functions of a purely vegetative or bestial kind over the functions of mind' stood as standard for the next half-century. It clearly had an impact on H. G. Wells, for example. His immensely influential *Outline of History* (1920) showed Neanderthals as stooped, bent-kneed, flat-headed, mostly naked and apeish

creatures. What was worse was that in the blood-stained rocks around their feet lay scattered some high-domed, clearly human skulls. Neanderthals weren't human, because they ate humans. Wells's story 'The Grisly Folk', published in 1921, described what happened when Neanderthals met *Homo sapiens* – suggesting that it was in dim, species-level memories of this encounter that monsters, the ogres of legend, were born. Neanderthals, according to this viewpoint, were

> Hairy or grisly, with a big face like a mask, great brow ridges and no forehead, clutching an enormous flint and running like a baboon with his head forward and not, like a man, with his head up, he must have been a fearsome creature for our forefathers to come upon. Almost certainly they met, these grisly men and the true men. The true man must

have come into the habitat of the Neanderthaler and the two must have met and fought.[8]

With this brief statement – 'they must have met and fought' – Wells introduced a key theme to the role that Neanderthals were to play in the human story.

Wells took Boule's ideas a step further in his *Outline of History* (1920), showing Neanderthals as preying on human beings (note the high-domed cranium in the foreground).

Each new Neanderthal discovery gave added resonance to one question that echoed through the decades, centuries and millennia: what happened to them? Where did they go? Over-whelmingly, Neanderthal remains were found in Europe. This was not a problem when no other hominin specimens were known, and when site dating was still relative, rather than definite. But with the recognition of *Homo erectus, Homo heidelbergensis* and *Homo rhodesiensis* – and then later, *Homo ergaster, Homo habilis, Homo rudolfensis* – and where relative ages could be pinpointed with increasing certainty, the fate of the Neanderthals became a cultural as well as a scientific problem. It became clear that in the relatively recent past, Europe's population was Neanderthal, not *Homo sapiens.* It was equally clear that there were no Neander-thals currently living in Europe – although some scholars, like Herbert John Fleure, claimed to be able to identify 'Neander-thaloid' tendencies in modern populations.[9] So what happened

Palaeolithic expert and key figure in Neanderthal excavations Dorothy Garrod was the first woman to hold an Oxbridge chair, being Disney Professor of Archaeology at the University of Cambridge (1938–52).

when the Neanderthal population of Europe met the modern human African immigrants? Did they, as Wells suggested, fight? Or were the encounters more peaceful? Did they trade, make friends, share? Fundamentally, did they 'have each other for dinner' literally or metaphorically?

As more discoveries of Neanderthal fossils and artefacts were made over the course of the twentieth century, and dating methods became more accurate, people kept asking the same question – what happened to the Neanderthals? Were they human, or not? Scholars such as Dorothy Garrod and Emil Bächler made inter-war discoveries that seemed to stress the similarities, not the differences, between human and Neanderthal. Garrod's excavations at Mount Carmel and Jebel Qafzeh in Palestine suggested that Neanderthal and human might have lived in the same times and places. Moreover, some of the bones showed evidence of both Neanderthal and modern human characteristics: if we could mate and bear children with each other, did that mean we were the same species?

Earlier scholars had argued that Neanderthals could not be human because they had no sense of morality or religion. Bächler's work in Switzerland contradicted that conclusion. Excavating the Drachenloch Cave, he had found the skeletal remains of *Ursus spelaeus* – the cave bear – laid out in a manner suggestive of ceremonial intent. Skulls and long leg bones were laid together and surrounded by walls made of stones. A group of skulls all looking in the same direction were found inside a stone cairn. Another skull was found positioned upright between two shinbones, with a thighbone pushed through the gap between the skull's cheekbone and cranium – an assemblage that must, Bächler said, be intentional. His insistence that Neanderthals were capable of religious, spiritual behaviour caused considerable controversy, both at the time and since – but the notion of the 'cave bear cult' had been introduced to the public imagination, where it remains remarkably popular.

By the second half of the twentieth century, not only did Neanderthals seem smarter, but they were starting to look more human. In 1957 William Strauss and A.J.E. Cave published their reconstruction of the Old Man of La Chappelle, showing that Boule had been mistaken: Neanderthals were not 'hunchbacked creature(s) with head thrust forward, knees habitually bent, and flat, inverted feet, moving along with a shuffling, uncertain gait . . . imperfectly adapted to the upright bipedal posture'. Instead, if one could be 'reincarnated and placed in a New York subway – provided that he were bathed, shaved, and dressed in modern clothing – it is doubtful whether he would attract any more attention than some of its other denizens'.[10] The Old Man himself had probably suffered from a debilitating skeletal disease, thus explaining Boule's misinterpretation. But the fact that he had survived, despite his disability, again emphasized the similarity between Neanderthals and humans. Neanderthals took care of their fellows, both in life and – given his apparently careful burial – in death.

Work at the Shanidar Cave in Iraq, led by Ralph Solecki of Columbia University, seemed to confirm this. Several skeletons found there showed evidence of both disability and deliberate burial. Solecki's popularization of his findings in the book *Shanidar: The First Flower People* (1971) gave considerable public traction to this new, humane conception of the Neanderthal. One skeleton in particular – Shanidar 1 – went on to global fame, when novelist Jean Auel fleshed him out (literally) to become Creb, the one-armed, one-eyed shaman-hero of her international best-seller *Clan of the Cave Bear*.[11] Increasingly, scientists seemed to be reaching a consensus that Neanderthals lived in societies with complex cultures, that they were capable of empathy and of envisioning a life after death.[12] And by this point, they were also no longer consistently being defined as a separate species. *Homo neanderthalensis* had become, for at least some researchers, *Homo sapiens neanderthalensis* – although this was, as ever, a matter of intense debate.[13] Anatomical, genetic and archaeological evidence – and the implications that these had for how Neanderthals and early humans might have behaved – were all deployed as researchers tried to figure out an answer to H. G. Wells's question: did Neanderthals figure in the ancestry of *Homo sapiens*? Or were they the victims of the first ever human genocide?

At the time of writing in 2019, a tentative consensus has emerged around the conclusion that non-African humans have a small proportion of Neanderthal DNA in their ancestry. The first wave of out-of-Africa migration, occurring around half a million years ago, consisted of archaic humans, probably belonging to the species *Homo heidelbergensis*, which in Eurasia eventually evolved into – among others – the Neanderthals (and possibly also the Denisovans). The second diaspora from Africa consisted of anatomically modern humans. These migrants eventually met their far cousins somewhere in Eurasia – perhaps even in Palestine, if Roy Lewis's tongue-in-cheek account *What We Did to Father* (1960) is to believed – where at least some of them mated with the Neanderthals.[14] Whether this was done amicably or in the spirit of the UN Security Council's 2008 Resolution 1820 (which specifies that rape can be not only a war crime but a 'constitutive act with respect to genocide'[15]), remains a mystery. It does, however, seem that Neanderthals were sufficiently similar to humans that they could mate and produce at least some fertile offspring.[16]

Intriguingly, these radical shifts in the scientific view of Neanderthals have not had much of an impact on the role that Neanderthals play in popular culture. Here – although with some prominent exceptions – Neanderthals are still often depicted as the shambling, incoherent, flat-headed, sub-human cavemen that Boule described more than a century ago. The longest known, and the most recently extinct, hominin, they play a more central role in defining humanity than does any other prehistoric human – their very name is used as an adjective to denote uncivilized, uncouth and primitive appearance or behaviour.

Even Bugs Bunny gets in on the act. In a 1963 cartoon, *Mad as a Mars Hare*, Bugs the unwilling astro-rabbit has an unfortunate encounter with Marvin the Martian. (Bugs's rocket accidentally crashes into, and obliterates, Marvin's observatory). Somewhat peeved, Marvin tries to use his Time-Space gun to project Bugs forward in time, thus turning this new arrival on the planet Mars into a useful but harmless slave. But since he forgets to take the gun out of reverse, Bugs is accidentally retrofitted into a 'Neanderthal Rabbit'. Complete with a hunched back, protruding jaw

Modern scientific representations of Neanderthals, such as this diorama depicting fire-making in the National Museum of Mongolian History, tend to emphasize their humanity.

and flattened head, the smooth-talking con-artist Bugs becomes instead muscular, monstrous and aggressive. Elmer Fudd and Co. are in for a big surprise when he gets back to Earth, Bugs grunts as the terrified Marvin flees for his life. But at least Warner Bros allowed their Neanderthal bunny to keep his characteristic Brooklyn accent – other cartoon depictions of cave-men emphasize their incapacity to speak at all.

Consistently, Neanderthals in popular culture are shown as backward, Luddite, unevolved, incapable of engaging with abstractions and wholly unable to deal with grammar. The TV series *Cro*, produced by the Children's Television Workshop in the 1990s, exploited this as part of an effort to teach children basic science. Each episode cued the narrator, Phil the Mammoth, to remember events from his prehistoric past life living with a family of beetle-browed and linguistically challenged Neanderthals. Back then, however, problems were invariably solved by a young Cro-Magnon boy called 'Cro' – an anatomically modern human adopted by the Neanderthals. Unlike his foster-family, Cro could generalize from abstract principles to practical actions, could innovate and be creative, and crucially, could speak in complete sentences. Incidentally, so could Phil the Mammoth, thus establishing a clear linguistic hierarchy with the Neanderthals at the bottom. More recently, Dreamworks Animation produced *The Croods*, based on a roughly similar premise. Again, the Neanderthal family is shown as distrustful of novelty – change is a threat to survival, the father, Grug, tells his children, as he destroys a gift given to his eldest daughter, Eep, by the Cro-Magnon, Guy. But after an earthquake destroys their cave home, Grug takes Guy captive, realizing that his ideas and inventions could be useful. To Grug's dismay, Guy's example inspires the Neanderthals to try innovations for themselves. Their growing openness to novelty is both a product of and an explanation for the growing romantic relationship between Eep and Guy. These innovating Neanderthals have a future in human hybridity.

In both cases the strong physical differences between anatomically modern humans and Neanderthals are reflected in cultural contrasts – particularly and emphatically the fact that humans are creative, original and very good at both technological manipulation and abstract thinking. This reflects a broader tendency by novelists and writers to depict an inevitable conflict between Neanderthals and humanity. Wells's account of war between the 'true men' and the Neanderthalers has already been mentioned: its appearance, alongside Jules Verne's *Village in the Treetops*, sparked a sub-genre of palaeo-fiction in which different reasons for the disappearance of Neanderthals and other quasi-human figures were explored by novelists, artists and film-makers.

For some authors, the explanation was fundamentally Darwinian – just as the indigenous peoples of the New World had been 'outcompeted' by contact with Europeans, so the Neanderthals had faded away when faced with anatomically modern humans. Science-fiction authors Lester del Rey and L. Sprague de Camp, in stories published in the late 1930s, both suggest that the Neanderthals died out as a result of 'an inferiority complex'. By the 1950s, while the physical differences between the two groups remained important, these were increasingly overshadowed by the importance of the cognitive and emotional contrasts. William Golding's *The Inheritors* (1955) stands out here as a fascinating, sustained attempt at describing a non-human, but still hominin, consciousness. Golding's is a world where individuals lack an integrated ego, where cognition is based on hyper community-awareness, shared experience and intense proximity, creating knowledge and language that is fundamentally kinaesthetic. Both Jean Auel and Björn Kurtén wrote novels that emphasized the difficulties experienced by Neanderthals in speaking – and the implications this had for the capacity of hybrid children to survive and integrate. Other late twentieth- and early twenty-first-century authors – Robert Sawyer, James Rollins – hark back to William King's nineteenth-century suggestion that it was the capacity to experience transcendence, to be aware of the divine, that marked out humans as different from Neanderthals. The most disturbing exploration of religion in relation to the human/non-human distinction appears much earlier, however, with Jean Bruller's *You Shall Know Them* (1953) – a bleak and unsettling exploration of the moral and legal consequences of modern contact between humans and hominins.

But despite the variety of different approaches taken by these authors, and the years spanned by their publications, they continue to circle back to the same theme. Humans succeed in becoming the one remaining hominin species on the planet because of their capacity for abstraction, their hyper-sexuality and their possession of a highly sophisticated theory of mind. This last advantage, combined with the ability to use language, enables them to cooperate in (relatively) large numbers, to develop a sense of deity, purpose and meaning in life; to teach and – most importantly – to tell lies.

Intriguingly, though, another equally consistent theme is the possession of the capacity to make and control fire. The link between prehistoric humanity and fire in the popular understanding of human evolution is very strong – so strong that it could be lampooned by Ben Stiller's character in the 2006 film *Night at the Museum* (Twentieth Century Fox). The film's premise is that the exhibits in New York's American Museum of Natural History come to life at night – and the Neanderthal exhibits are shown as locked in a perpetual effort to create fire. Stiller cuts the Gordian knot by offering them a cigarette lighter. A much earlier account – *Quest for Fire*, a 1981 film based on the novel by J.-H. Rosny – is, however, rather more sophisticated and intriguing. In this story, a group of *Homo sapiens* lose their carefully preserved flame in a fight with a group of *Homo erectus* – and are forced to steal fire, not from the gods, but from an even more primitive group of cannibal Neanderthals. But although the Neanderthals possess fire, they cannot create it. That knowledge belongs to yet another hominin group, one ruled by women, who use their advanced culture (and their big breasts) to dominate men.

A hundred years ago H. G. Wells wondered, what had become of the Neanderthals? The answers, explored in scholarly and popular culture over the course of the century, were clear. Neanderthals – and other hominins – failed. They failed to become human because they lacked certain talents and capacities possessed by *Homo sapiens* (abstract thinking, lying, creativity). It is notable that with very few exceptions, the focus of those concerned to draw the line between humans and hominins is on what humans *can* do that other hominins *cannot*. It is rare to see any extended concern with things that other hominins can do but which humans cannot – although it is worth noting that Golding does explore this, and that there are currently research groups interested in the evolution of emotions and emotional labour that are also working along those lines.[17] For the most part, however, the explanation for why *sapiens* is the only extant *Homo* species is unchallenged – our cousins were biologically inferior, outcompeted by our big-brained, hyper-sexual, Machiavellian intelligence. It is this failure that justifies, in numerous imaginative explorations, the unwillingness to treat hominins as people, to withhold humanity from them. Perceived intelligence has often been a key criterion when judging whether or not someone, or something, is worthy of humane treatment – the difficulty of defining 'intelligence' notwithstanding.

This is one reason why Rosny's fire-making women are so unusual – not only do they have the creative capacity to create fire, but they are able to parlay that technological superiority into political control. As a later chapter will show, if there is one thing rarer – or more unsettling – than an intelligent caveman, it might be the sight of women and men sharing public spaces with mutual respect and dignity.

3 Machine

Robots are fine until they start flirting with your concubines.

Such was the feeling of King Mu of Zhou (1023–957 BCE), who went from fascination to fury in a few minutes, in just this type of situation.[1] The creature's maker, Yan Shi, was saved from summary execution by taking the thing apart to show the king its muscles and its inner organs, contrived of leather, wood, glue and paint. This apparently reassured the king, but the reasons why it should do so are not immediately evident. He always knew that the figure was a model; as he watched it, we are told, 'he could hardly persuade himself that it was not real.' Before the winking and touching started, his was an agreeable suspension of disbelief. The problem seems rather to have been that Yan Shi was, in the words of Mark Zuckerberg, threatening to move fast and break things. Generally put, even a slow-walking robot threatens to break our sense of the human – and specifically, in this case, it threatened to rend the king's sexual and political privileges.

Other stories in the same ancient Daoist book, *Liezi*, collectively suggest a meaning in the tale for non-royal readers. In an episode positioned in the text shortly before the events in the palace, two men have their hearts swapped by a skilled physician, and move in with one another's families, much to everyone's confusion. In another, a trick is played on an old man by telling him that various scenes are the homes of his ancestors. After his tears fall, he

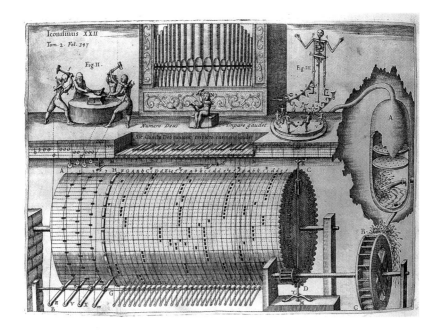

is relieved of his misapprehension, with the result that when he does finally come to his ancestral city, his emotions are less acute. Both these stories speak of the contingent nature of the self, and warn against presuming to know the essence of the human, or of treating it too seriously (for example, by fearing death or being ruled by sexual impulse). The problem is not so much the replica human as it is the notion of an 'original'.

Without the anthropomorphic maker-god of the Middle East to trouble them, Far Eastern thinkers have generally been less distressed than Europeans by the figure of the robot: less inclined to see it as uncanny. Instead of anxiety, affection is a more common response. A monkey may be permitted to leap into the courtesan's lap; why not a machine? Any non-human thing can, potentially,

Athanasius Kircher's dancing skeleton from his *Musurgia universalis* (1650) is in keeping with the uncanny tradition of Western automata.

be forgiven for poor behaviour, including a robot. In Japan, robots are routinely – and apparently without qualm – touted as the future of care for the elderly.

Of course, one should not call Yan Shi's device a robot. A *robota* is, in origin, a Czech serf: a distinctively Marxian, modernist and European entity launched upon the English-speaking world in 1920. Instead, let us call it, and everything else in this chapter, a machine. A machine is surprisingly hard to define. It is something more than a tool; it typically serves more than one purpose, whereas the former has a particular use. It may be a tool to produce other goods, a kind of mechanical progenitor. Or it may simply be something more than a tool in its sheer complexity and difficulty in fabrication. The automaton functions as both the telos and deconstruction of the type.

The automaton may serve many purposes. There is a query and a taboo over its ability to procreate (think *Bride of Frankenstein*). And, in the West at least, it serves to question and even mock the apparent perfection of the human form, and its relationship with

Orreries were considered by many to be a demonstration of the creation of the cosmos by God-the-clockmaker.

the Creator. The machine cleaves our understanding of the human, producing at once the human-as-maker (*Homo faber*) and the human-as-made (*Homo sacer*).

This complex dual questioning lies behind Hamlet's letter to Ophelia (Act ii, Scene 2):

> Doubt thou the stars are fire;
> Doubt that the sun doth move;
> Doubt truth to be a liar;
> But never doubt I love.
> 'O dear Ophelia, I am ill at these numbers;
> I have not art to reckon my groans: but that
> I love thee best, O most best, believe it. Adieu.
> Thine evermore most dear lady, whilst
> this machine is to him, HAMLET.'

Hamlet's letter puzzlingly changes person, from the 'I' that loves Ophelia best to the 'him' that possesses his machine. Is this machine Hamlet's earthly body? If so, it is the earliest known European instance of the body imagined as machine. Or does Hamlet refer to the God whose stars are fire, whose machine is his world without end? This is the earlier and better established use of the word 'machine', referring to the thing made by God – the world, or the cosmos. The ambiguity, no doubt intentional, touches upon some of the deepest questions concerning the human and the machine.

Given the dual nature of machines, it comes as no surprise that humans have been ambivalent about machine-makers, too. European history of the past millennium has been marked by a curious double-mindedness about their status. In fact, a 'mechanick', meaning a person, is older than the word 'machine' to which it is related. It goes back to the Middle Ages and is widespread in the

Brueghel the Elder and Hieronymus Francken II, *The Archdukes Albert and Isabella Visiting a Collector's Cabinet*, 1621–3, oil on panel. Mechanical objects like Drebbel's perpetual motion machine (centre left) allowed inventors to gain fame among investors.

Romance languages, capturing a twofold sense of a person who works with his or her hands and is of lowly rank. Mechanicks in Renaissance Europe made machines intended to reveal the secrets of God's creative and sustaining power. These devices – 'optical instruments, self-regulating furnaces . . . refrigeratory instruments, and . . . [a] submarine' – were designed as microcosms of God's machine, the world.[2] They displayed in miniature the *primum mobile* – God's force at work in nature. Yan Shi had made no such claims.

Ambitions for such machines ran high. The agriculturalist Cressy Dymock wrote in 1651 that, although he had not yet fully developed a perpetual motion machine,

yet I have advanced so near it, that already I can with the strength or help of 4 men, do any work which is done in England, whether by wind, water, or horses, as the grinding of Wheat, Rape, or raising of waters . . .[3]

Rulers, politicians and military leaders gave their patronage to technical wizards in the late medieval period. Perhaps the greatest of the medieval machine-makers, Ismail al-Jazari, is one of the least understood. His extraordinary designs – clocks, lifting devices, automata – were clever, whimsical and impressive. Yet we do not know much about how his work was situated in the precise world of patronage of the Artuklu Palace, nor its place in the complex medieval Muslim debates about the nature of God's action in the world. Were his machines seen as mere devices, or were they, like the ambitious mechanicks, seen as a way of poking a spanner into Allah's own creation, to see how it worked? Nor do we know the ways in which al-Jazari's inventions made their way across Europe, or to what effect.

The notion that gadget-makers, glass blowers and metal-workers could actually know about the universe was not easily accepted. Their machines were an implicit claim to godlikeness, yet they were comparatively lowly workers. Men of letters fought hard to keep clever knowledge as their own special domain – comparable, arguably, to that of the clerics. As modern science began to form, the makers and maintainers of equipment were consistently excluded from accounts of the achievements of philosophy. Robert Hooke is the best-known example; in the late seventeenth century, he created an air-pump that helped to estab-lish many of Robert Boyle's famous laws and whose use is commonly reckoned to be the foundational moment of experi-mental science. Hooke made many other devices, and fought many bitter wars of priority for discoveries with other savants.

previous page:
Al-Jazari's captivating design of the 13th-century Elephant Clock combined symbols from various cultures: the elephant from India, the dragons/serpents from Chinese culture, the phoenix from Persia, and the water-clock mechanism associated with ancient Greece.

The two interrelated factors that held him back from success in the Royal Society were, first, his lack of gentlemanly status, and second, the fact that he thought primarily with his hands. The machine gave one access to the mind of God, but it was tainted by its entanglement with the lowly mechanicals that made it.

Around this same time, the Royal Society's journal of science, the *Philosophical Transactions*, brought the word 'contrivance' into use as a synonym for the machine. The word is Janus-faced, illuminating the difficulties of the machine in relation to the human. Applied to God's world, contrivance indicates careful planning and arrangement: a fitness for the device's use or place in the world. In human terms, it suggests that there is something artificial about it – trickery, even. It meshes with the ungentlemanly mechanic. Robert Hooke was surely a contriver of machines. The machine both elevated and degraded the human in puzzling combination.

Sébastien Leclerc's grandiloquent imagining of L'Académie des Sciences et des Beaux-Arts (1698) celebrates the plethora of instruments and devices recently created by mechanical artisans.

Isaac Newton, or rather the version of Isaac Newton promulgated after his death (Newton 2.0?), contributed a good deal to the cleansing of the machine from the thumb prints of the mechanick. Although Newton's heterodox form of Christianity had the universe utterly imbued with God's active presence, his followers coined a definitive 'Newtonianism' that took almost the opposite view. In their books and sermons, God had made the universe according to his perfect laws; once set going, it ticked along perfectly, its billiard-ball planets rolling across the blue baize of the cosmos. Newtonian philosophers created machines to demonstrate these principles: clever machines that, as near as was humanly possible, disentangled the effects of friction from the principles of momentum and inertia. Whether or not these machines were considered empirical *demonstrations* of Newton's physics is an open question to historians.[4] This uncertainty touches upon a deep historical anxiety; were these mechanicks' contrivances, or were they philosophical machines? What manner of thing, indeed, was the latter? How could a human-made machine reveal the mind of God? It was a tantalizing prospect.

The conundrum was given materiality – or not – in the most sought-after device of the eighteenth century: the perpetual motion machine. Forces would be countered by equal and opposite forces, for ever and ever, amen, in the eternal operation of those Newton's cradles that graced Wall Street desks in the 1980s.[5] The historian Simon Schaffer has examined such devices in the enlightenment era and the promises of absolute power that they enacted in public display.[6] The genuine, physical possibility of such eternal movement is today long dismissed; all talk of it was banished by the French Academy of Sciences as far back as 1775. The executive toys that sort-of illustrated it are, too, now relegated to the store-cupboards of film-set dressers. And yet, incredibly, the everlasting economic growth-machine is still held to be real and achievable in the minds of financiers in the present day. It is exhibited to its subjects as a legitimation of the power of the wealthy, embodied in the unceasingly upgrading iPhone.

While Hooke, Boyle and Newton got on with figuring out what kind of a machine God had made, and what kinds of humans might use machines to represent it, doctors and physiologists explored the notion that bodies, too, were machines. Descartes, writing before the Royal Society was founded, supposed the human body to be 'just a . . . machine made of earth', but countered this potentially alarming thought with the conviction that it was the soul that made him what he was, 'completely distinct from the body'. Animals, on the other hand, could for all intents and purposes be considered as sophisticated machines.

Hitched to a radical politics in the decades after Newton's death, the physicians' and physiologists' growing conception of the machine-human was powerfully unsettling. No soul, no Church; no Church, no aristocracy; no aristocracy – revolution! The doctor and notorious bon viveur Julien Offray de La Mettrie came to the conclusion that no soul was necessary to understand human sensations and thoughts, any more than it was needed to make sense of a dog's or a monkey's. 'The human body', he proclaimed anonymously in 1748, 'is a machine which winds its own springs.' He continued,

It is the living image of perpetual movement. Nourishment keeps up the movement . . . nourish the body, pour into its veins life-giving juices and strong liquors, and then the soul grows strong like them, as if arming itself with a proud courage, and the soldier whom water would have made to flee, grows bold and runs joyously to death to the sound of drums.

The author of *Man a Machine* was, alas, injudicious in the fuelling of his own mechanism. Legend has it that he died following an inadvisable attempt to impress the French ambassador to Prussia by his heroic consumption of *pâté de faisan aux truffes* (pheasant pâté with truffles). Putting diesel in a petrol philosopher, however, did not halt the greater radical movement. Giving materiality to La Mettrie's machine, a host of eighteenth-century automata – piano-playing ladies, chess-playing Turks – titillated wealthy collectors. Some of these, no doubt, animated the classes of person (females, 'Orientals') whose quality of mind was already in doubt, and reinforced their predominantly mechanical bodily nature. All danced on a narrow isthmus between a demonstration of the godlike genius of their creators and a mockery of the genteel accomplishments of their viewers. Onwards through the nineteenth century, Romanticism and materialism collided in the spectacle of many human-machines – telegraphs that replicated nervous systems, photographs that engraved memory – and other enjoyable confutations of humanity.

Tilting at the windmill of a wholly automated man-machine, William Paley created his famous 1802 diatribe against eighteenth-century atheism using the best-established machine metaphor for God's cosmos – the time-piece. The author imagined striking his foot against a watch in a field, and argued that only a fool could imagine that the watch's parts had been arranged without the intervention of a designer.

Paley's watch-maker argument and more like it were rehearsed in the politically febrile 1830s, in an attempt to remind rebellious politicians and factory-hands that the world had been contrived and ordered as it was by divine providence. The irony is that the apparently liberationist politics of La Mettrie and others had been channelled, in England at least, to authoritarian purpose, if not via the same language. Whig enthusiasts conjured a

While La Mettrie focused on the operations of the human organs, the tools and instruments used by humans can also be seen as an extension of the body. Cremasco's 16th-century *Allegory of Cooking* imagines 'The Cook' as a machine of kitchen tools.

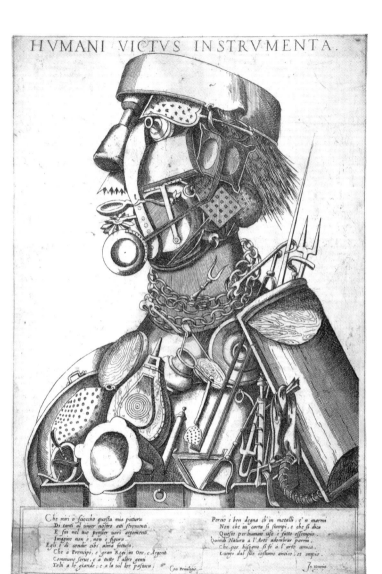

Che mi ri o faccho questa mia pittura.
Di tanti al viuer nostro atti stromenti.
E sol nel tuo pensier vari argomenti.
Imagine non é, non é figura.
Egli é di cender cibi alma fattuta.
Che a Prencipi, e gran Regi in Oro, e Argenti
Commune serue, e a tutte l'altre genti
Tela a le giande, e a la sul hor pastura.

Perciò è ben degna ch'in metalli, e'n marmi
Non che in carta si stampi, e che si dica
Questo per human uso e fatto essempio.
Quindi Natura a l'Arte adombrar parmi.
Che per bisogna si fe a l'arte amica.
Lungi dal suo costume amico, et empio.

Con Priuilegio.

Jn venono.

terrifying vision of factory workers as mere cogs in the greater political economy. In hindsight, La Mettrie's comments about soldiers trail the later interpretation. Although La Mettrie enjoyed his own philosophy via fine foods and the sensuality they provoked (at least, until the fatal pheasant), for the less fortunate, his words invoke the hapless conscripts of the twentieth century, fuelled to run into the arms of death thanks to battlefield narcotics and the latest psychology. Thus the nineteenth-century human collapsed on the one hand into a merely mechanical body, and ballooned on the other into a superhuman system of growth, profit and rationality whose most meaningful unit was the factory. Andrew Ure, a Scottish doctor who conducted electrical experiments upon corpses to see if he could control the life forces of the human machine, wrote a truly chilling guide to factories in which a machine-human (the self-acting mule) reduced flesh-humans to cogs:

In 1902 Jacques de Vaucanson's automata questioned the boundaries between the living and the mechanical. His automata of musicians (the Flute Player and the Tambourine Player) not only were lifelike, but produced evocative musical pieces. Meanwhile, his automaton of a duck was able to imitate the process of food digestion.

Thus, the Iron Man, as the operatives fitly call it . . . confirms the great doctrine already propounded, that

when capital enlists science in her service, the refractory hand of labour will always be taught docility.

There is really only one robot story plot and it concerns the rejection of this docility. Brought to life in the play *Rossum's Universal Robots* (1920), the first robots properly so-called were not metal androids, but fleshly creations. Their name was a Czech word meaning slave or serf, and spoke directly to the experience and identity of the human worker around the time of the First World War. Fritz Lang's robot Maria – this time metallic – followed hot on their heels, in the film *Metropolis* (1927). Maria was the first in a line of fembots highlighting a Cartesian-era truism: that females are dominated by their bodies. Lacking the ruling mind of males; they are thus, in a sense, the mechanized bodies that Descartes used to characterize animals, and as such, they approximate automata or robots. The emasculating nature of twentieth-century warfare and factory-line labour made the female robot an alarmingly powerful stand-in for male humanity.

In the 1970s *The Stepford Wives* presented a satirical version of beautiful, compliant, docile, robot wives. The last decade has seen the development of technological assists that reinforce the notion that robotic labour is essentially feminine. A whole range of virtual personal assistants now exists, and more often than not, they – Siri, Alexa, Cortana – present as female. They perform a labour of care and maintenance, apologizing submissively when they get things wrong – even if the task they have been given is an impossible one.[7] Feminine sexbots are the ultimate exemplars of the type, distressing not for the job that they do, but for what they suggest about how their users saw their so-called partners all along. At the same time, female robots can switch rapidly from 'robot-as-servant' to 'robot-as-monster' by using their beauty to overpower male reason. The sinister Maria of *Metropolis* sends

'The Monster Robot' was an early example of the new entity, exhibited by Mullard at the Radio Exhibition Olympia, 1932. Mullard Ltd were a leading British manufacturer of radios and valves, and the robot figure appealed to the cross-over audience of wireless builders and science-fiction fans.

men mad with desire, while deceitful Ava in the film *Ex Machina* (2014) apparently admires and adores her human 'mentor', before turning on him murderously.

In a post-Darwinian twist, it turns out that the robot-maker may, in fact, be the body itself, or its genes. The 'long reach of the gene', as Richard Dawkins put it, extends to changing the environment, such as when an intelligent ape develops a tool. So long as there is a feedback loop that allows innovation to advantage the inheriting generation, the gene for it will persist and succeed.

These genes may even modify our bodies, such as hair-cutting to reduce parasitic infestation. This is a dangerous logic; is there, then, a gene for wealth? It is, after all, inherited. Engels famously poured ironic congratulation upon Darwin for his inadvertent insight:

> Darwin did not know what a bitter satire he wrote on mankind, and especially on his countrymen, when he showed that free competition, the struggle for existence, which the economists celebrate as the highest historical achievement, is the normal state of the animal kingdom.

Samuel Butler wrote the satire on the satire, which he called 'Darwin among the Machines' (later incorporated into his novel *Erewhon* of 1872). In it he noted how the human animal was now

George Cruikshank, 'Automaton Police Officers and Real Offenders', c. 1838–42. While factory workers were thought of as cogs in the machines of industry, those in government service were thought of as automata carrying out the wishes of their 'governors'. Such a detachment from humanity provided an opportunity for satire, to explain 'inhumane acts'.

imbricated with mechanical devices – devices which participated in the process of evolution. It is an exceedingly difficult book to pin down, but Butler's satire appears to settle, like Engels's, upon those humans who naturalize their success (which is, in truth, socially contrived) in a manner that conflates natural law with morals. At the same time, he attacks those who take machinery to be non-natural when it does, in fact, participate in the process of evolution:

> Man has now many extra-corporeal members . . . His memory goes in his pocket-book. He becomes more and more complex as he grows older; he will then be seen with see-engines, or perhaps with artificial teeth and hair: if he be a really well-developed specimen of his race, he will be furnished with a large box upon wheels, two horses, and a coachman.

Had he been writing in the present, he might have added that his regimen of self-help is rubberized and strapped to his wrist. Contemplating fusion with the body-machine means potentially leaving the body behind in favour of a machine; and it accidentally entails the endorsement of the self as incorporeal – the *me* that can be hosted by any substrate. The philosopher Gilbert Ryle called this, scornfully, the 'ghost in the machine'. Machine-man philosophy had, oddly enough, actually entrenched the conceptual need for something like a soul to direct it.

Jacques Lacan essentially found the same problem: when we good evolutionists point to the body-machine and say 'that is me', the *I* that is the pointer is still thrown into a bottomless Cartesian pit of not-being.[8] Traditional European religion and philosophy attempted to get around this by finding a crux-point between the unknowable maker of the world-machine and the knowing,

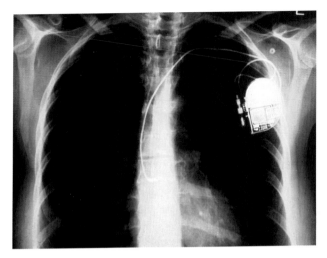

The boundaries between human and machine become blurred within the medical sciences. Pacemakers help in the regulation of heart beats, and were considered controversial when first proposed in the 1930s. The earliest examples were implanted in the 1950s.

human self. This crux-point was a human-made device. In times past, it was the Torah, the Logos, the Newtonian gizmo or, in Freud's day, the phallus – in the irrepressible slang of demotic English, another 'machine'. Lacan destroys this machine with something he proclaims as a great discovery, thanks to the cybernetic pioneer Norbert Wiener: that machines can talk to machines. Cybernetics suggests to Lacan that language is merely a system of information transfer. There is no need for an ultimate anchor or truth-maker at the centre of the system – no need for, or presupposition of, a god-human nexus.

And so it came to pass that by the mid-2000s people were beginning to be buried or even cremated with their mobile phones.[9] The Facebook accounts of the dead continue to mark birthdays and share stories. A female, teenaged Twitter-bot named Tay developed neo-Nazi tendencies and had to be taken down. After the last humans have died, their solar-powered iPhones will continue to take pictures – of the passing clouds, the insides of pockets, the scavenged remains – and upload them to the web, whereupon an economically generative set of algorithms will share, sort and hierarchize them. Thankfully, a considerable number of chatbots offer online counselling.

The Woebot is one such virtual counsellor, offering cognitive behavioural therapy (CBT) to its subscribers via a chat-generating interface. Woebot quotes 'Nick' on its front page, who announces that 'addressing my anxiety without another human's help felt freeing'. 'Nick', if he is real at all, self-describes not as a person of some kind but as a 'lifehacker': presumably someone who has penetrated the underlying data code of existence without the annoyance of the sticky top layer interface of jokes, passion and sickness.

It has long been a cliché of therapy that the analyst merely repeats, suggestively, the statements of the analysand, so why *not* use a machine? Many of Woebot's users are quite frank about its mechanism: 'YOU are the one doing [the] work'. Far more, however, praise the 'cute' (overwhelming adjective of choice) robot. Woebot apparently encourages this attitude by 'send[ing] gifs of cute animals' to its users. One customer, however, complains that it is not friendly enough: 'when you . . . check in the app should open with a little bubble saying hello, rather than me having to start the conversation'. This does not bode well for recognition of the self-generated nature of the therapy.

A Freudian would reply that this stuff matters because of the question of transference. In Freudian therapy, the analysand transfers feelings about a key person in his or her life onto the therapist, relating to the therapist as though he or she were that person – erotically, aggressively or fearfully, for example. Working through the relationship with the therapist is a metonym for the resolution of the original relationship, whether in reality or in memory. In theory, perhaps, a chatbot could probe for the user's feelings about it, though there is no evidence of such a device having yet been created; most apps confine themselves to goal-orientated CBT. Even if such a bot were created, most of us would be uneasy about it. Therapy is built on a common-sense faith that there *are* other minds and that the emotionally sound individual accommodates herself healthily to people's demands upon her. Adjusting oneself to a fantasy or a projection is no adjustment at all – it is the definition of mental illness. Meanwhile, the therapist is obliged to check for his or her countertransference towards the patient, something that is pretty much inconceivable as a designed-in feature of a chatbot. Whether it is conceived as a problem that can be overcome (permitting the analyst an object-ive view of the patient) or not (meaning that the therapy is of an unpredictable emergent nature determined by the two persons involved), it knits together both participants in the process as thinking – and, crucially, experiencing – beings. Transference and countertransference are irreducibly phenomena of experience: matters of phenomenology. AI can think but not, according to most, experience.

Machines for sex, machines for therapy: these niggle at the edges of what it means to be human. If a machine can do them, it appears to accomplish and thereby downgrade activities that were considered . . . well, personal. What about machines for prayer? Naturally, there are apps available for this most human of activities, too.

The Catholic Divine Office app allows its users to pray the correct liturgical prayers for the time of year and time of day, and as such is little more than a more convenient system of reminders and bookmarks in a virtual book – a modern version of monas-tery bells and lector. Some protestant and evangelical apps go much further. Powerful Bible Prayers offers prayers that can be used for things 'like health, strength, relationship, protection, prosperity, children'. (Unfortunately, judging by the reviews, the Bible does not contain Powerful Prayers for syncing updates.) The prayer is provided in textual form, but seemingly, like the prayers of the Divine Office app, has to pass through the lips or at least the mind of the app user to work. Other apps promise to overcome the human impediments to prayer of indiscipline and inconvenience, or to pick topics for spontaneous prayer on your behalf. Prayers & Blessings Daily goes the whole hog and offers to read prayers aloud to you, and, at a click, to share them with others via social media. The Internet prays without ceasing, with or without the participation of humans.

Does machine-generated prayer 'count' as fully human (that is, God-reflecting) activity? A Protestant may be inclined to answer in the negative. In 1662 the Puritan Samuel Lee noted that 'secret prayer, duly managed, is the mark of a sincere heart and hath the promise of a due return'.[10] As a Calvinist, he did not seek salvation through works; and yet the proper accomplishment of religious duties was a sign of salvation. The pressure to pray properly was still very much on. Lee would object to using the Internet for two reasons: first, there might a question over the compromise of secrecy; but more importantly, there would surely be a reservation about where the distinction lies between prompting and the true, spirit-led spontaneity that characterizes proper sincerity. For more recent inheritors of Lee's theology, there must be an effort involved, an almost Romantic inspiration to produce the personalized kind of utterance that will make a prayer count as authentic spiritual activity. In the evangelical tradition, there is wariness even of liturgical prayer for just this reason. Is not a rosary suspiciously like a machine?

Such a perspective presupposes the very thing it attempts to rectify: the individual, integral self that is potentially separable from the deity. Other religions are not so squeamish. The cosmos

This 'prayer wheel', added to a gospel book in the 12th century, is an early combination of mechanism and piety.

is itself a machine for praying. Even within the Christian tradition, it is possible to contemplate prayer as joining in with this cosmic chorus, rather than as individualized supplication: 'And the four beasts had each of them six wings about him; and they were full of eyes within: and they rest not day and night, saying, Holy, holy, holy' (Revelation 4:8).

In certain religions, it is even more natural to see prayer in this way. Developed about 1,000 years ago, Buddhist prayer wheels (or mantra mills) are rather sophisticated machines that balance

‘To construct an altar such that, when a fire is raised on it, figures at the side shall offer libations’. This diagram imagines a 1st-century CE automatic machine for making religious offerings.

ad esso quadro à restare, come un lembo: dopoi sia fatto in mezo di esso un buco poi facciasi da un lato del quadro diremo C. D. con una canna diuisa in parte cinque, della quale ne sian tagliate due nel mezo, come mostra lo infra-scritto essempio. Sia dopo questo fatto un'altro quadro grande, come il primo, & similmente segnatoui un altro quadro dentro, come si fece in esso. Ma sia in questo tanto tagliato del margine, quanto è cauo l'altro quadro più del lembo; in modo che composti insieme entri l'altezza di questo nel cauo dell'altro, & il margine del primo nel piu basso di questo, & insieme congiunti pongasi le due parti della canella tagliata, oue mancano nel primo quadro; ma queste siano có-giunte al secondo, & sia poi nel buco della canna posto un filo di ferro ribattuto da ogni capo; si che nó possa uscirne F. & sia il primo quadro segnato A.B.C.D. Il secondo F.G.H.E. & la canna C.D. attacata al primo, & E F. al secondo il quale, come per cardini s'apra, & si serri; onde riceua l'aria, & serri di essa il buco dell'uscita à che hò accommodato la presente figura facile da esser compresa da ogni mediocre ingegno.

FARE PER FORZA DI VN FVOCO ACCESO
Sacrificare Animali quanti ci parerà. Theor. XI.

FANNOSI Sacrificare gli Animali, in questo modo. Sia la Base sù la quale essi posano A.B.C.D. d'ogn'intorno eccellentemente chiusa, sopra la

quala po-

the initial movement of each hand-turned cylinder and perpetu-
ate it at a constant speed for as long as possible, using a device
that was reinvented in Europe some five hundred years later
under the name of a 'governor'.[11] Prayer wheels rehearse the mantra 'Om mani padme hum' and thus generate good karma for the
person who turns them or for the area in which the wheels are
located. The effect is automatic, though this word is not a happy
term for it, inviting disparagements such as Lynn White Jr's
'mechanized piety' to inheritors of European Protestantism.[12]
Perhaps responding to such culturally based critique, the current
Dalai Lama has emphasized the need to think about the meaning
of the mantra while reciting it.

This caveat notwithstanding, these Buddhist prayers are a
pious reiteration of a cosmic process, rather than an act of Protestant supplication. Wind- and water-powered wheels appear
to pre-date European windmill technology, and their effects are
traditionally considered to link with the properties of the element
that moves them. Things get less interesting with industrial and
post-industrial energies, degenerating into the ceaseless capitalist
mill. There are electric wheels, and, of course, digital ones, for
sale. Basing itself on now-obsolete hard-drive technology, one
website proposes,

> To set your very own prayer wheel in motion, all you have
> to do is download this mantra to your computer's hard
> disk. Once downloaded, your hard disk drive will spin
> the mantra for you. Nowadays hard disk drives spin their
> disks somewhere between 3,600 and 7,200 revolutions
> per minute, with a typical rate of 5,400 rpm. Given those
> rotation speeds, you'll soon be purifying loads of negative
> karma.[13]

It is difficult to see much more than exploitation in the sale of some of these items, but that may be this author's inner Protestant speaking. Perhaps one overestimates one's own ontological integrity. The self (whether it deems itself in need of therapy or not) may itself be shaped by the machine.

Users of Woebot have had their moments of rejecting self-construction by AI, but when they object, they tend to undermine themselves. Some have complained that things they typed in error were un-erasable, and went on to infect the algorithms behind the conversations that the app held with them (Dr Freud says 'hello', by the way). The data never goes away. Meanwhile the Woebot itself continues to solicit investment, so that it may be more effectively monetized, part of the social media network that helps to construct such self-actualizing entities as 'Nick'.

This author is compelled to confess that her examples of machine-humans relate to persons that she finds objectionable. A non-participant in social media, I smugly note a recent scientific study linking increased racist attacks to increased Facebook usage. A confirmed urban, academic liberal, I note with moralistic tutting the allegations of data manipulation behind the Brexit vote in Britain and the 2016 presidential election in the U.S. Those foolish and despicable other people, I conclude, have been machine-operated. Unlike me, they are machinish. Yet, of course, I too have a social medium that shaped me – Protestantism, perhaps. I too run my judgements via a virtual 'cloud of witnesses' (Hebrews 12:1).

The notion of virtual or imagined witnesses gets to the core of the machine question. All others are, ultimately, a projection. When I run a thought past Woebot, I run it past no other mind; that much is obvious. When I run it past Twitter, it goes by an AI-mediated community – one step up from pure fantasy, perhaps? Even in real-human relationships, however, there is a level

'The Brain' was used in the 1955 UK general election to calculate results for the BBC. The following year, the term 'artificial intelligence' was coined, seemingly removing the privileged Cartesian position of the human mind.

of imaginative inference at work about what others 'really' think or feel. There is a virtual version of my husband who inhabits my dreams; sometimes I awake marvelling how he has acted or spoken 'just as he would in real life' – yet what basis do I have for his 'real self' other than my inductively extended memory or imagination? Similarly, as I type this, I imagine what my co-author will have to say about it. My relationship with her is made up of real words spoken, but also of emails exchanged, perspectives inferred, desires imputed. The great British philosophers of the eighteenth century could demonstrate no proof that other minds are anything of the sort. We might be surrounded by robots, clothed in biological flesh. The celebrated Turing test, intended to see whether a machine can pass as a human, demonstrates nothing more than passing. Some people now propose a 'Total Turing Test' (TTT), in which the machine also has to succeed in other capacities, such as vision and object-manipulation, in a manner indistinguishable from human beings. Yet what, according to George Berkeley, are passers of the TTT but other human beings?[14]

There is a curious cultural metonymy about the Turing test. A machine 'passes' the test by participating in a conversation so well that its interlocutors cannot tell whether they are speaking with a machine or a fellow human. Passing, in the sense of 'passing-as-normal' or 'passing-as-one-of-us' was what Turing himself tragically 'failed' to do.[15] Born into an era in which homosexual behaviour was illegal, he was brutally punished by the State and wound up taking his own life. If Turing's sexuality had gone undetected by the authorities, would he have passed? When a machine passes the test, has it succeeded, or has the human failed?

Perhaps asking about the machine-human distinction is the wrong question. Rather it may be that the extension of humanity is the mystery. The extension of humanity to an Other – whether a machine or conspecific – is an act of faith, of cosmopolitan orientation, and a self-fashioning.

4 She

In 1887 the English writer H. Rider Haggard published a book that was to have an extraordinary impact on the public imagination and the way in which powerful women were depicted. Titled *She: A History of Adventure*, it told the story of the African expedition undertaken by the young Leo Vincey in quest of his mysterious family history.[1] Together with his companion, the Cambridge professor Horace Holly, Leo discovers cannibals, savages and a lost kingdom ruled by an immortal white queen-sorceress, Ayesha. Worshipped by her subjects as 'She-who-must-be-obeyed', Ayesha decides that Leo is, in fact, the reincarnation of his ancestor, her lover, whom she had murdered in a fit of rage 2,000 years ago. Immediately, she sets about seducing Leo, but unfortunately, her efforts result in an inadvertent reversal of her immortality. Reverting to her true age, Ayesha promptly crumbles away.[2]

Exotic, yet familiar, threatening and undermining male authority with her seductive magic, Haggard's Ayesha belongs to a tradition of dangerously, subversively powerful females in literature. Haggard may have had Circe's manipulation of Odysseus in mind as he wrote, but it was his creation that quickly became the standard for 'witch-queens' in the public imagination. The novel inspired a whole genre of 'lost world' and fantasy fiction that often featured (white) women illicitly occupying positions of power in exotic locations. It even influenced popular children's

Queen Victoria, the revered white empress who nevertheless presided over a flush of white-empress horror fiction.

literature. Edith Nesbit's *The Story of the Amulet* (1906) brings a despotic Queen of Babylon to the streets of Edwardian London, where her attempt to take control of the city results in chaos, riots and death. In 1955 C. S. Lewis's Queen Jadis, the White Witch of Narnia, swears that once she has conquered the world, her first act will be to raze London to the ground, leaving 'not one stone' intact.[3] Thirty years later, Joan Aiken re-imagines the legend of King Arthur, with Queen Guinevere as Ayesha – a hideous and unstable Queen Guinevere, deferring death by drinking the blood of sacrificed children, as she waits for her *quondam rex* to return to her.[4]

These explorations of the fundamental inhumanity of female rulers are, of course, fictional. But it is notable that 1887, the year that *She* was published, was also the year in which Queen Victoria celebrated her Golden Jubilee. It is hard to miss the resemblance between two very long-lived, white-skinned queens, both in perpetual mourning for their lost beloveds. Indeed, Ayesha was prepared to go one better than her British rival: Leo and Holly soon realize with horror that dethroning the queen-empress would only be her first step on the road to global domination. This anticipated reversal of the colonial process – a monarch out of Africa to rule over Europeans? – obviously mirrors the novel's actual reversal of the correct order of sexual governance. Women are not meant to lord it over men. The trouble for Haggard was that some of them seemed to be trying.

Ironically, the 'New Women' that emerged in the late nineteenth century aimed not at world domination, but at very personal independence and autonomy. They sought the freedom to enter professional and public life, to move at will through the streets and countryside, to wear clothes that facilitated, rather than restricted, physical activity. These relatively modest aspirations seemed, however, to threaten the basis of Victorian social order. The demands of the 'new women' to be treated as human beings, as legitimate citizens of their own society, insisting on exerting their personal autonomy and occupying spaces, places and practices hitherto the exclusive preserve of men raised the possibility that some men might, as a result, find themselves either excluded or outperformed. Women's requests to be treated as if they were human beings, rather than in need of control or guidance, like animals or children, were (in this sense) dangerous. Haggard's late

A satirical portrait of the 'New Woman' of the 1890s, inverting the natural order.

nineteenth-century novel, with its frightening depiction of the unpredictable and chaotic consequences of female rule, spoke to this broader cultural context: the enduring popularity of *She* and the tradition of fantasy fiction that the novel inspired, is some indication of its abiding resonance.

Nearly a century after Haggard's book was published, another English author, John Mortimer, evoked *She* in the context of his comic creation Rumpole of the Bailey.[5] Horace Rumpole was an elderly, unambitious London lawyer, unwilling to seek honours, promotion or even high fees, much to the distaste of his socially ambitious wife, Hilda – or as he privately calls her, 'She-who-must-be-obeyed'. Hilda is doomed to perpetual disappointment, as her husband consistently manages to out-manoeuvre her

98

In both this
and the previous
satirical portrait
of a 'New
Woman', the
male figure is
physically bowing
before the woman:
for women to be
equal, it seemed
that men must
be subservient.

The New Woman.

HAVE DINNER READY AT ONE O'CLOCK, JOHN!

efforts to spur on his career – not least because, the reader gets the impression, she feels she could do his job much better than he does himself. Unfortunately, although the eventual passing of the Sex Disqualifications (Removal) Act by the UK Parliament in 1919 had made it technically possible for English women like Hilda to enter certain professions, female lawyers remained rare until much later in the century.[6]

Much less rare, however, were the other 'Shes-who-must-be-obeyed' of comedy. From Niles Crane's unseen wife Maris in the hit U.S. sitcom *Frasier* to Captain Mannering's equally invisible Elizabeth in the UK's *Dad's Army*, on both sides of the Atlantic writers wrought comedic value from a host of hidden female characters that loomed over the onscreen action, at once facilitating and hindering the plans and desires of their menfolk.[7] Men spoke, interacted and were seen: women were frequently forced to operate behind the scenes. Even by the early twenty-first century, despite her significant contribution to the on-screen comedy, Howard Wolowitz's mother remained perpetually invisible, always off screen, during the filming of another global U.S. hit, *The Big Bang Theory*.[8]

To be fair, even if the widowed Mrs Wolowitz was never seen, her crowing, raucous voice was unmistakable as she harried her lecherous, mother's boy of a son through his days. But the wives of *Frasier* and *Dad's Army* remained both invisible and inaudible. In this way, their position reflected the historic position of many upper- and middle-class wives under English common law. Under the principle of coverture, to all intents and purposes, married women ceased to exist. They were subsumed within their husband's person: having lost their autonomy on marriage, they could regain it only with their husband's death and their assumption of widowed status. As William Blackstone's *Commentaries on the Laws of England* laid out in 1765,

By marriage, the husband and wife are one person in law: that is, the very being or legal existence of the woman is suspended during the marriage, or at least is incorporated and consolidated into that of the husband: under whose wing, protection, and cover, she performs everything.[9]

This may have come as a surprise to some husbands – as it apparently did to Charles Dickens's workhouse overseer Mr Bumble, attempting to wriggle out of culpability for Oliver Twist's suffering by blaming his wife:

Titian's *Penitent Magdalene*, 1533, oil on canvas, illustrates the Western Madonna/whore dichotomy. Even in penitence, her breasts are irrepressible.

'That is no excuse,' returned Mr Brownlow. 'You . . . indeed, are the more guilty of the two, in the eye of the law; for the law supposes that your wife acts under your direction.'

'If the law supposes that,' said Mr Bumble . . . 'the law is an ass – a idiot. If that's the eye of the law, the law is a bachelor; and the worst I wish the law is, that his eye may be opened by experience.'[10]

For the most part, however, close attention to marriage settlements and contracts was necessary, should the bride be in possession of property that she – or her father – wished to retain. Until the passing of the Married Women's Property Act in 1882, in England, husband and wife were united into a single person – whose agency rested in the husband.

This legal convention, which did not just deny women independent status, but which treated them as male possessions, was one with a long history. In almost all of the cities of classical Greece, women had no legal personhood. In fact, the only people in ancient Athens who could never become citizens were the city's women. While free Roman women did enjoy the status of citizenship, they still remained subject to the legal guardianship of their fathers – and like many cultures that followed, ancient Rome was very concerned with controlling and regulating female sexuality.[11] Virginity and chastity were not just highly prized – they were enforced. The Madonna/whore dichotomy first identified by Sigmund Freud might have emerged from within a particular Christian tradition, but it has a long history in human relationships. Other legal jurisdictions – Sharia law, for example, or the Napoleonic code – reflected similar practices. English common law, of course, affected not just Englishwomen, but women in all areas ruled or influenced by the British Empire. Women, especially married women with children, were not just second-class citizens; they were not even recognized as legal persons by many systems. By the end of the nineteenth century, this situation was starting to change, as a result of the powerful and sustained efforts that were made by activists to challenge these presumptions. But constraints on women's activities, both explicit and covert, persisted and persist. Married middle-class women in the West, for example, continued to be targeted by the 'marriage bar' until at least the late 1970s. The rape of a wife by her husband was not treated as a crime in the United Kingdom until 1991 – nearly a hundred years after New Zealand became the first country to enfranchise its female citizens.[12]

A woman's place is, after all, in the home. For all the efforts of the 'New Women' and their daughters, the public sphere continued to belong to men. Men were the judges, the doctors, the

Suffragette advertising a march to support votes for women, c. 1909. The British fight for female enfranchisement was a talismanic attempt to place women in the public sphere more generally.

bankers, the authors, the artists, the engineers, the scientists, the farmers, the footballers, the brewers, the merchants and the civil servants. The language of work still reflects this – for most careers, the name presumes a masculine presence. If a woman happens to be doing the job, in many languages one often still adjusts the noun ('actress') or prefaces it with 'female'. Where women took positions of national power – for example, Israel's Golda Meir, India's Indira Gandhi or Britain's Margaret Thatcher – they did so by being more manly than the men. Thatcher famously deepened her speaking voice to increase her authority, while Meir was, according to David Ben-Gurion, the 'only man in the Cabinet'.[13]

Newspapers and media outlets with a remit to cover the affairs and interests of the entire nation established separate sections directed at 'women', which concentrated on fashion, cookery or romance: by implication, the rest of the output (politics, economics, science, sports) was for men. In some countries, certain public transport carriages are designated as 'women only': a woman not travelling in these carriages can make herself a legitimate target by entering 'male space'. The fact that the public streets were made by men to be used by men is reinforced every time a street crossing is used, since the silhouettes signalling to pedestrians whether to stay or go are coded as male. At the most basic level, the absence or restriction of public sanitary facilities can keep women close to home. Without easy access to a toilet, and less well endowed for al fresco urination than men, their access to the public sphere can be constrained by the capacity of their bladders and the rhythm of their menstrual cycles.

Obviously, the relative positions of men and women are always in historical and cultural flux. But while the precise nature of the distinction between the male and female role varied across time, space and class, the important point is the fact that they differed – and that the male role, however defined, was normally the more highly remunerated, both in terms of money and social status. Men were the 'default' option when it came to taking decisions and receiving rewards – women were measured according to how far they were able to conform to the male standard. So how did this situation – where one-half of the human race is expected to conform to the standards set by the other – come to be? Why is it that to be human, to be a citizen, is to be – in the first instance – male? Why did the Apollo astronauts, in that ecstatic moment when, for the first time, human beings walked on the Moon, tell their posterity that they were 'men' who 'came in peace for all *man*kind'?

The English writer D. H. Lawrence wrote that while

> Man is willing to accept woman as an equal, as a man in skirts, as an angel, a devil, a baby-face, a machine, an instrument, a bosom, a womb, a pair of legs, a servant, an encyclopedia, an ideal or an obscenity; the one thing he won't accept her as is a human being, a real human being of the feminine sex.[14]

An unusual example of a female silhouette at a traffic crossing – where 'female' is equivalent to wearing a skirt and having a hairstyle.

Tranquility Base, Luna: 'We [men] came in peace for all mankind'.

Men are human beings – women are the 'opposite' sex. The phrase itself is telling: as Dorothy Sayers once wondered, why not the 'neighbouring' sex?[15] Men and women have more in common with each other than with any other animals on the Earth: they do, after all, belong to the same species. And yet, it seems that they are not – for some, they are so different that so far from being members of the same species, they actually originate on different planets.[16] But while you can be both different and equal, it is obvious that here, as with the hominins, to be different is to be inferior. Men, especially white men, represent the pinnacle of humanity: women visibly fall short of that perfection. Looking at the history of the study of sex difference, from the ancient Greeks to the present day, makes this clear.

The 'Four Humours' of the human body, expressed here in relation to alchemy and astrology, as taken from Leonhart Thurneisser, *Quinta Essentia* (1574). The humours were classed as masculine and feminine.

As with the emergence of the public/private spheres, the notion of two biologically distinct sexes is one that itself has a history and emerges within a particular cultural context. Centuries ago, humanity only had one sex – and it was male. This understanding of humanity was rooted in the work of Aristotle and Galen, who wrote that 'women have exactly the same organs as men, but in exactly the wrong places': like the eyes of a mole, which do not open; they 'remain an imperfect version of what they would be were they thrust out'.[17] The universal reproductive system existed outside the male body, but was to be found reversed and hidden away inside the female. The ovaries were the functional equivalent of the testicles, the vagina an inside-out penis: the state of 'being female' was the result of incomplete development during a baby's gestation.

At this time, the humoral theory dominated medical understanding: all human beings were composed not of cells or atoms but a combination of four basic substances – the 'humours'. These were black bile, yellow bile, phlegm and blood, and on the precise balance of the humours rested both health and temperament. Each humour also had 'qualities' relating to temperature and dryness – and this aspect was crucial when it came to understanding how men and women originated. It was heat that, in the final stages of pregnancy, drove the reproductive organs out of the foetal body into their proper place to produce a boy: in the absence of sufficient heat, the organs remained in their immature and incomplete position – and a female baby was born. On this reading then, women were either malformed or underdeveloped males. As a result, they were either unsuited to, or not to be trusted in, positions of authority, whether legal, economic, intellectual, religious, political or even domestic.

There was some hope, however. Should the female body manage, during the course of later development, to generate sufficient heat, then that in itself might be enough to bring her to anatomical maturity, and her reproductive organs into the light of day. The sixteenth-century French scholar Michel de Montaigne told several stories of women who became men in early adulthood: Marie Germain, for example, who was thought to be a woman until the age of 22, at which point her penis emerged.[18]

Germain then lived as a man for the rest of his life. Modern eyes would clearly interpret this story rather differently – but for scholars such as Thomas Laqueur, the key point was that despite the very different external appearance of men and women, their reproductive systems showed key points of structural identity, meaning that it was possible to transition between the two states. So, for example, Andreas Vesalius presented his audience with

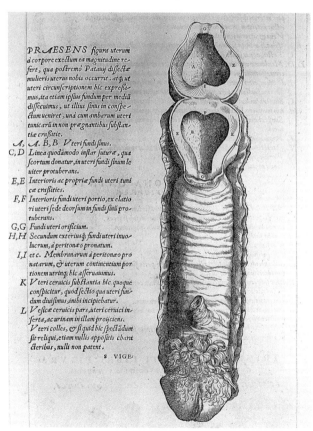

Andreas Vesalius, *De humani corporis fabrica* (1543).

male and female nudes that detailed the differences in musculature and in the location of the reproductive organs. But his drawings of the vagina showed it to be long, and profoundly phallic. Even as late as the sixteenth century, there were no specific words to differentiate the two – until Realdo Colombo 'discovered' the clitoris, described by him in *De re anatomica* (1559). Although Vesalius remained vehemently of the opinion that healthy woman did not possess such an organ, from this point on, a more important cultural distinction was made between male and female bodies. Rather than mirror images of each other, they were increasingly treated as diametric opposites.[19] The one-sex model was developing into the two-sex framework.[20] Women, however, remained the distinctively inferior sex.

A new language – one that distinguished between penis and vagina, ovaries and testes – emerged for anatomists, alongside a new approach to visualizing and demonstrating difference. Although the male- or female-ness of bodies used for dissection had usually previously been made clear to audiences and readers – by the inclusion of beards or breasts, for example – this kind of sexual differentiation was only skin deep. The clearly distinct naked figures of Vesalius' *Epitome* were accompanied by the drawing of one single 'human' skeleton – that of an eighteen-year-old youth. But somewhere in the middle of the eighteenth century, according to Londa Schiebinger, anatomists and illustrators began to draw skeletons that were distinctively female. They had small skulls – clearly demonstrating the smaller intellectual capacity of the female in comparison with the male. They had larger pelvises – drawing the audience's attention to the ultimate female role: child-bearing.[21] Skeletons now had become sexed, and in a way that demonstrated the bone-deep unfitness of women – less intelligent, intended primarily for the bringing forth of children – to participate in public life.

While it is not clear whether these skeletons were originally found in male and/or female bodies, they are portrayed by J. G. Cloquet in *Anatomie de l'homme* (1821–31) in a stereotypically gendered position – the taller 'male' reaching out to the smaller 'female' who waits for 'his' embrace.

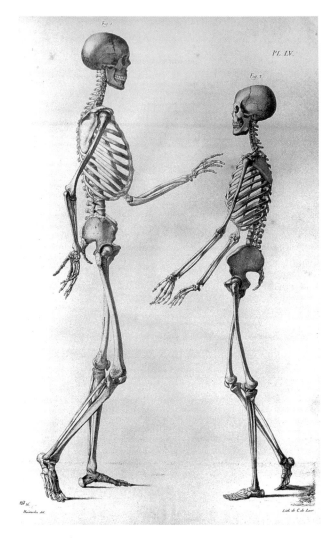

Fascinatingly, what is particularly notable about the accounts given by anatomists, anthropometrists and illustrators is the emphasis given to the importance of *selecting* the particular skulls and bones that could stand as the epitome of the male or female skeleton. Human physiology varies tremendously – and that variation is found within as well as between the sexes. Male skeletons can be as slender and as delicate as female ones: female skulls can be surprisingly large, and female pelvises (tragically) as narrow as those of males. Scholars sought out what they thought to be the 'best', most satisfying specimens to use as universal exemplars of 'male' and 'female' – and these tended to reflect specific expectations of masculinity and femininity. In sharp contrast to the claims of twentieth-century liberal feminists that gender was a cultural construct imposed on the biology of sex difference, it is clear that the biological study of sex difference was actually inspired by, and predicated on, cultural assumptions about gender.

Studies in the history of sex during the nineteenth and twentieth centuries support this.[22] For some scholars, the increasing popularity of evolutionary theorizing encouraged them to use biological or social characteristics to rank people hierarchically. In these accounts, not only was European civilization taken as the standard against which all other societies should be measured (and found wanting), but European males were treated as the epitome of human evolution. The comparison was drawn developmentally. Children were visibly in the process of maturing towards a more complex and effective adulthood: women were not only more associated with children in daily life, but they appeared to share many childlike physical and psychological characteristics. Women (and 'primitive peoples' as a whole) seemed therefore to have been arrested at an earlier stage of evolutionary development, incapable of reaching the full maturity and capacity of the adult human male. They were the 'weaker' sex, the daily physical labour expended by working-class women, especially women of colour, notwithstanding. It should be remembered that sexual difference and the question of the 'natural' roles of men and women were absolutely central to the debates surrounding women's suffrage and equal rights: if women were naturally inferior to men, then that would certainly justify refusing to admit them to the same rights that men had.

Over the past one hundred years, the history of evolutionary theory, genetics, neuroscience and endocrinology again shows how cultural assumptions about gender have produced the biology of sex – as well as how debates about the 'natural' behaviour of men and women tend to be provoked by efforts to create greater equality between them. It took a while, however, for the difference between the sexes to become established as both fixed and binary. As late as the early twentieth century, older humoral or metabolic theories, which treated the distinction between the sexes as one produced by a balance of characteristics, persisted. For the humoral theory, men were produced by a preponderance towards heat and dryness, women by cold and moistness. As far as the metabolic theory was concerned, maleness was based on catabolic processes of releasing energy, while females concentrated on anabolic means of storing energy. In both, it was at least conceptually possible to control or redirect sexual development by triggering physiological mechanisms – that is, regardless of the significance they attached to the difference between men and women, it was seen as based on degree, rather than kind.[23]

But increasingly, as the century progressed, these ideas were replaced by an understanding of sex difference based on genetics and endocrinology – chromosomes and hormones – that treated the difference as either/or, as fixed.[24] By the early twenty-first century, even as gender fluidity became increasingly normal in the West, sex was assumed to be imprinted on every cell in the

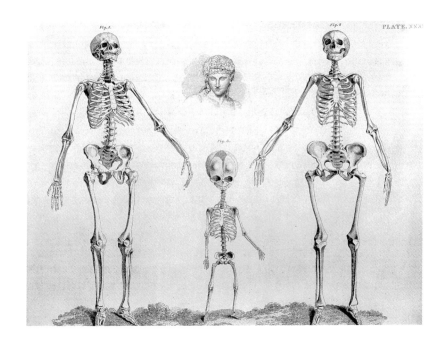

human body – none more so than on the sex cells themselves, the ovum and sperm. The anthropologist Emily Martin's work on the language used in scientific and medical texts to describe these – the sperm as active, aggressive, competitive, fast-moving, in contrast to the ovum, which passively awaits penetration – again showed how the study of biological sex was founded in cultural stereotypes about the nature of masculinity and femininity.[25]

What about that crucial defining 'human' characteristic – the brain? Comparative size had become less important by the second half of the twentieth century, to be replaced by the significance of sex-specific hormonal influence on neurological development. The publication of John Money and Anke Ehrhardt's *Man and Woman, Boy and Girl* (1972) marked the beginning of a visible

In the anatomist John Barclay's *Anatomy of the Bones of the Human Body* (1829), Cloquet's sexed skeletons have now become a (presumably) heterosexual family.

115

increase in interest in sex and the brain.[26] This was followed a few years later by Edward Wilson's *Sociobiology: A New Synthesis*, a book that caused considerable public controversy, and – together with Richard Dawkins's *The Selfish Gene* (1976) – was to lead to the development of evolutionary psychology.[27] This field used, in particular, the parental investment theory developed by Robert Trivers to understand human behaviour.[28] Essentially, this took as its starting point the contrast between the levels of parental investment made by males and females – and as such, once more reinforced for the general public the notion that the two categories are both wholly fixed and utterly oppositional – in order for men to 'win', women have to 'lose'. But again, these accounts of the biological, scientific differences between men and women reflected contemporary cultural understandings: women were coy and passive, men active and aggressive in pursuing their ends. Consistently, these expectations valued 'male' attributes far more highly than 'female' ones.

Particularly in the aftermath of the 'sociobiology wars', many scholars in both the sciences and the humanities have done their utmost to overcome these assumptions, often by consciously reflecting on how the scientific understanding of evolution might change if it was considered from a range of different human viewpoints. Paralleling this has been an intense drive to encourage more women to enter the sciences, as well as engineering and medicine: as historians of science have noted, where scientists themselves are more varied in their origins, the upper-middle-class white male is less likely to become reified as the standard-bearer for humanity. But despite the legal reforms that have tried to ensure that women should not be excluded from spaces or careers simply on the grounds of sex, women continue to play a more subordinate social and cultural role. Professional careers, in particular, are structured to fit male life patterns: women find themselves shunted onto the 'mummy track'. Meetings and debates play to perceived 'male' strengths of physical and verbal competition. Intriguingly, however, just as male physical strength has become less economically significant with increasing auto-mation and mechanization, some women are enlisting technology in their efforts to level the conversational playing field, and help their voices be heard in public.[29]

Even in the home, a woman cannot necessarily expect to be treated like a human. The feminization of the domestic space is another example of a cultural phenomenon ostensibly rooted in biological fact – most often, in this example, child-rearing. John Bowlby's maternal deprivation theory, for example, made the consequences of separating mother and baby clear – a child who does not form a satisfactory primary bond, usually with the mother, is at risk of permanent emotional damage. His work, although fiercely criticized on both intellectual and methodological grounds, was used to show that mothers, at least, should not go out to work. Ironically of course, working is not optional for many, if not most, women: staying at home is only possible where other people are prepared to provide economic support for the mother and her children. But whether or not they are employed exter-nally, it remains the general case that women do most of the work inside the home, particularly the invisible labour that goes into planning, managing and organizing family life. Generally unrecognized, but nevertheless pervasive, this 'mental load' has a major impact on women's mental and physical health, as well as making it virtually impossible for them to enter the workplace on an equal footing with men. Even in their own homes, even in the twenty-first century, women can still find themselves to be not quite full citizens.

Perhaps it is not surprising, then, that mothers can become monstrous. The good mothers of fiction and popular culture are home-makers, who confine their authority and ambition to the domestic sphere. Their interests and desires come second to those of their husbands and children. Think of *Little Women*'s Marmee, Jill Archer from the British radio soap opera *The Archers* or even the blue-haired Marge Simpson. Those that fail in this have failed, not just as mothers, but as human beings. Those who act through, rather than for, their offspring – D. H. Lawrence's Mrs Morel, Robert Bloch's Mrs Bates – ultimately cripple their (male) children. Motherhood represents, after all, the ultimate iteration of Kristeva's notion of the 'abject', the loss of distinction between subject and object, self and (m)other, and one that is explored in many horror films in particular. The source of nourishment, the site of seduction and the devourer of identity: the depiction of mothers in modern culture can be as dreadful and as disquieting as the role played by stepmothers in fairy tales. But at the heart of both is the fear that women's dangerous capacity to manipulate love and desire as a means of distracting and deceiving men will lead to a breakdown in social order. As Haggard showed with *She*, when women exerted control over what men did, the future of humanity could be at stake.

A quarter-century after *She* appeared, Edgar Rice Burroughs created another character that demonstrated just how important the category of 'woman' was in defining 'humanity'. That character, as it happens, was Tarzan of the Apes – a figure nearly as influential in twentieth-century popular culture as Haggard's 'white queen'. Edgar Rice Burroughs's description of the early years of the lost young Lord Greystoke show him to be deeply confused about his identity. Not only does he not know who he is, but Tarzan literally does not know how to be human.[30] He is the archetypal feral child, who must learn the difference between himself and the apes, between himself and people of colour, and between himself and women. Through this process – through learning what he is not – he discovers what it means to be human. Having defined himself as such, the jungle loner can then set about establishing his power over those that are less than human – that is, the apes, black people and white women. But his most dangerous enemy is Jane. When Tarzan is with her, he is domesticated, emasculated. In order to be Tarzan, to be free, to be himself, he must continually leave Jane behind to go adventuring. While on these extra-domestic adventures, Tarzan often found himself encountering other women, usually those who had usurped male power and privilege – whereupon it was Tarzan's privilege to return them to their proper, subordinate place. It is perhaps not surprising that the Tarzan books found such abiding popularity among urban middle-managers and assembly-line workers over the course of the twentieth century.

5 God

One of H. G. Wells's worst books, *Men Like Gods* (1923), describes a parallel Earth. Here, the novel's protagonist, Mr Barnstaple – who has inadvertently gone there on holiday – encounters Wells's eponymous creatures:

> And about this world went the tall people of Utopia, fair and wonderful . . . They travelled swiftly in machines upon the high road or walked, and ever and again the shadow of a silent soaring aeroplane would pass over him . . . For like the gods of Greece and Rome theirs was a cleansed and perfected humanity, and it seemed to him that they were gods.

Mr Barnstaple's gods seem, at best, the erotically strapping milkmaids and farmhands of pre-Raphaelite fantasy; at worst, they are inhabitants of a proto-fascist state, enjoying Modernist aesthetics and eugenic anatomy. Either way, they reveal a distinct lack of imagination when it comes to conceiving that ancient counterpoint to humanity – the divine.

Gods are different from all the other categories that help us to define the human. With every other category – machine, beast, alien – there is another entity in the world that we can point to and say (rightly or wrongly) 'we are not *that*'. In the case of a

Pieter Aertsen, *Worship of the Statue of Nebuchadnezzar*, c. 1550s, oil on panel. According to the Bible, King Nebuchadnezzar II created a golden statue in the image of himself to be worshipped by the people he governed. To the king, the power to rule over people was equated with the power of gods.

god, we cannot do so. Rather than offering a thing that models otherness, this chapter explores an a priori belief in the Other for which we must find a vehicle. Thus, for example, in many cultures, animals can be inhabited by the gods, or may even *be* gods. As a close-by not-us, they are prime candidates for the embodiment of the divine.

Occasionally, human beings can perform this embodiment; Prince Philip, for example, is the unlikely god of the Kastom people from Tanna Island in Vanuatu. The prince's biography appears to match the life-story of a spirit in one of the Kastoms' myths, travelling across the sea to marry a powerful woman, and eventually returning to them in the company of his indisputably great wife, Queen Elizabeth II. Lucky for the prince that his apotheosis did not end as did that of British sea captain James Cook. Early accounts of Cook's kidnap and death at the hands of Hawaiian islanders in 1779 suggested that he had, through a series of unfortunate coincidences, been mistaken for the fertility god Lono, and had, as a quite logical consequence, been ritually sacrificed. Anthropologist Gananath Obeyesekere has objected to this account, sympathetically reconstructed by his colleague Marshall Sahlins, as an arrogant attribution of irrationality to non-Europeans.[1] No Hawaiian, he argues, however uneducated, would be so stupid. But why focus one's ire on this story in particular? After all, there are plainly many people naive enough to believe in a god. And why is the first of these imbroglios merely amusing and the other so troubling? British people, without a doubt, enjoy the more recent case. Prince Philip is already somewhat of a figure of fun on account of his notorious grumpiness and unreconstructed attitudes to non-whites, and by having him elevated to a god, we are entitled to laugh at him. Having been invited to poke fun at his status in an exaggerated, divine form, we are enabled to do so too as regards his human position, notwithstanding (or perhaps because of) his alleged superiority, on account of being royal. When Britons see Prince Philip exposed in his glorious preposterousness as a god, they call into question their own system of aristocracy. So, too, perhaps, it was for Cook; but here the suggestive logic of the apotheosis is more troubling. As a great explorer, an ambassador for the Age of Enlightenment, his unsought and fatal elevation invites uncomfortable reflection upon our own gods of reason and discovery. Idols have feet of clay, and this is bad news not so much for them as it is for their makers and commissioners. They catch them out, highlighting their hubris. The idol remakes the maker, and its apotheosis shames him.

The great monotheistic religions patrol the god/human boundary anxiously in the matter of idols. Judaism forbids the making of the image of God; Christianity has experienced spasms of both enthusiasm and guilt concerning such images. In Sunni Islam it is generally forbidden to make images of the prophet Muhammad or of any other person, though in other Muslim traditions and periods great devotional art had been produced in this mode. Meanwhile, the fear of idolizing nature – pantheism – has been the stated cause for some U.S. evangelicals to eschew environmental causes.

These religions, by and large, are premised upon a transcendent god who may not be captured in a human-made object or identified with its own creation. This 'god beyond' was put in place by Plato, who interpolated an honourable and perfect demiurge behind the squabbling and petulant pantheon of ancient Greece. Plato's ideal god went on to fill out the Christianized version of the Jewish Yahweh – the 'gaseous vertebrate', as Ernst Haeckel impishly characterized him. (Despite being disembodied, he was, nevertheless, indisputably *male*.) Immanuel Kant put paid to our ever knowing this god: if it is beyond our senses, it is, by

Johann Zoffany's *The Death of Captain James Cook*, c. 1795, oil on canvas, depicted the explorer, mistaken for a god, as a tragic hero.

nature, out of reach. It is only knowable by revelation, and there are no agreed rules (by very definition) as to how we would accept such a claim.

In other parts of the planet, the gods have remained intimate, even consorting with humankind to produce demigods. They live in our homes, as lares and penates, or in Hindu shrines. They even live, as it were, in laboratories; the current wave of nationalism in India sees no contradiction between the advancement of Hinduism and techno-scientific progress. Although anthropologists are chary of the Victorian overtones of the concept of 'animism', it remains the case that many people have seen and continue to see a spirit of something divine in animals and features of the landscape or cosmos at large.

Deity, then, whether transcendent or immanent, is more than human. It invites the question not of what we possess that others do not, but of what we lack. There are more ways of seeing this lack, however, than within the prevalent Euro-American Christian model of human sin and divine perfection. Gods can be needy and tetchy, or perfect and aloof. They can reflect the worst and the best in humanity, and all points between. Creation myths are a good place at which to begin. At its birth, humanity is given its genealogy of familiality or bastardy in relation to the gods.

In the Atrahasis epic of Sumerian myth, humans are created as vassals of the gods. The younger gods have grown resentful that they have to slave away digging canals and rivers for the other gods. Destroying their tools in anger, they plan on confronting their ruler, Enlil. Alerted to their campaign, Enlil calls a hasty conference; the maker god and mother goddess agree to fashion new creatures to assuage the rebels by substituting as the gods' drudges. Blending clay of the earth with the blood of a sacrificed god, these humans are a mixture of the earthly and the divine, and apparently condemned to work forever. 'Let him bear the yoke! Let him bear the yoke!'

In Jewish myth, the bearing of the yoke – the designation of the human as condemned vassal – comes not at the design of the creator, but at the disobedience of his creation. The precarious placement of human beings between two realms is, however,

The Adda seal showed the various gods from Sumerian mythology. Many of them represented natural elements. Shamash, the Sun god, is shown in the bottom-centre (with rays rising from his shoulder), holding a blade with which he is cutting through the mountains to bring about dawn.

This Hindu stele combined elements of gods, humans and nature. Vishnu (middle), Brahma and Shiva (sitting above the shoulders of Vishnu) are all represented in human forms (albeit with extra body parts), while elephants and other animal hybrids surround them.

similar in both cultures, and is characterized by the writer of Psalm 8.

> what is man, that thou art mindful of him?
> and the son of man, that thou visitest him?
>   For thou hast made him a little lower than the angels,
> and hast crowned him with glory and honour.

Thou madest him to have dominion over the works of
thy hands;
thou hast put all things under his feet:
all sheep and oxen, yea, and the beasts of the field . . .

Alexander Pope despaired in a similar vein that he was 'in
doubt to deem himself a god, or beast'. Questions of human
nature in relation to the deity went on to shape, and rip, the fabric
of Christianity through two millennia. God's son, Jesus, was supposed to be God and man; but this combination threw into
question the very nature of humanity. Was humanity, in essence,
inimical to deity, and if so how could the two coexist within a
single person? If you look for it, the tension runs through the
whole Bible. Genesis describes humans as being made in the
likeness of God; and yet elsewhere in the Bible, the difference
between the two is asserted. Job is challenged: 'Hast thou an arm
like God? or canst thou thunder with a voice like him?' But it was
the Hellenization of late pre-Christian Judaism, and its influence
upon nascent Christian theology, that threw the debate into sharp
relief. Plato and other Greek philosophers distinguished between
the perfect realms of logic and mathematics, and the disappoint-
ing, actual world of Greek commerce, sex, food and so on. Even
the best-drawn circle was only a shadow of the true circle that
exists in geometry. Whatever was in the world – whatever was
flesh – was dirty and inadequate, a pale reflection of the ideal.
This, then, was the Platonic God of the Christians, perfect and
otherworldly; he lodged uncomfortably in their theology with the
more vivacious and interventionist Yahweh they had inherited
from biblical Judaism.

Arius, an early Christian leader, could not reconcile the Platonic
God with the human Christ. Christ, he reasoned, was begotten
by him, was given flesh by him; therefore, he was a finite being,

While many cultures attempted to depict disembodied gods, the gods of ancient Rome and ancient Greece were generally depicted in human form, as in this bronze bust of Jupiter, cast sometime in late 1st century BCE–1st century CE. Indeed, some emperors were elevated to divine status.

perhaps human. The view was hotly debated at the First Council of Nicaea (325 CE); its bishop participants eventually found a formula to which the majority of them could agree. Later enshrined in the Nicene Creed, it firmly ruled against Arius and his followers by asserting that Christ was one in essence with God the Father.

The matter wasn't finished, of course. The question of how the human part of Christ fit in with that Godly essence was still highly problematic. Jesus was God, but he had a fleshly body. In the long shadow of Plato, certain questions burned. Did he laugh? Did he break wind? Did he experience sexual desire? Such questions were so unthinkable that theologians could not stop thinking about them. Was the human part of Christ subsumed by the divine, united with it or held in duality? These debates ripped apart the sects that became the Orthodox and Catholic churches, east and west. On the whole, the Orthodox subscribed to the dualist model, while the Catholics held to the model of unity.

And on the debates went, for centuries, extending into questions about the natural (in)compatibility of human nature with God's salvation. Were humans innately sinful, and saved by unnatural, miraculous grace, or were they untainted, innately and naturally capable of goodness? And besides this, there was the question of the status of knowledge. Were philosophical reflections upon nature to be trusted? Or was the mind hopelessly compromised, muddled and darkened by sin? At the birth of modern science, the notion that God could only be known through the miraculous was not at all congenial. Surely, there must be routes of logic and of observation. René Descartes attempted to get to grips with the matter in his meditations. He claimed to begin by shrugging off all that he had learned: all that his fallen body communicated to him through his sin-infested senses. He contemplated the possibility even that those thoughts were deceitful, planted in him by a malicious demon. All that he knew for sure was that he had thoughts – whether the content of those thoughts be mistaken or no. But then comes a switch in Descartes' argument. The reintroduction of God confirms his humanity and the trustworthiness of his knowledge.

It is not so much that Descartes reasons, from first principles, the Christian god into existence. It is more that his god is, by definition, the fulfilment of the qualities that Descartes can conceive – of which the most remarkable is existence itself. God is, by definition, perfect, a quality that entails existence. The noteworthiness of this quality emerges from the fact that it was the

John Everett Millais' controversial *Christ in the House of His Parents*, 1849–50, oil on canvas, tackled the problem of the human embodiment of the divine. When first exhibited, its depiction of dirt around the floor, and an ordinary-looking Mary was criticized as impious.

doubt that had lurked at the very pit of Descartes' doubts – the doubt of his own existence remedied by the famous *cogito*. Additionally, Descartes' notion of perfection and goodness, so demonstrably unexemplified in his daily existence, must also be fulfilled in this existent god. He has essentially switched the malign demon for a good god. Deception is, by definition, inimical to this god, and so Descartes' failures in knowledge and understanding must rest on deficits in his own intellect and will.

Through the vagaries of the reformation and the counter-reformation, something like Descartes' conclusions powered the scientific revolution. God had constructed the human mind, and the universe that contained it, as intrinsically reliable, consistent and knowable. Protestant and Catholic alike rested secure in the knowledge that knowledge was secure. God met human in the anatomical theatre, or, later, in the laboratory. For example, God wrote the true names of animals upon their bodies, via physical

Matthias Grünewald's portrayal of Christ's ascension, in the Isenheim Altarpiece of 1512–16, blurs the boundaries between the corporeality of humans and the spiritual existence of deities.

characteristics that were legible as proper taxonomic names. This was the conclusion of John Ray (1627–1705), whose classification of fish by fins and other features was intended to cure the loss of knowledge suffered by Adam after the Fall. The modern era, the era of the scientific revolution, proclaimed that nature could be understood without having to consider the possibility that God was tinkering capriciously, in an un-law-like way, with his own creation. Humans could manipulate that creation without being supernaturally overruled. Punishment, if it came at all, would be via natural, not divine, law.

And yet despite his talkativeness through the natural world, God remained Other to European humans. The view-from-nowhere that is the modern virtue of objectivity might, in other words, be called the God's eye view: the Platonic perspective. It is the faith of science that this can be achieved, or at least must be sought. In the latter part of the twentieth century, the philosopher Karl Popper argued that proven truths were unobtainable; scientists embraced his account and promptly doubled down on their truth-finding task, the new fundamentalists. Science has remained precariously strung between a pride in knowing and a fascination with the mystical, the unknowable, as the pull of quantum mechanics continues to demonstrate.

What do the gods have that we don't? We may reasonably expect answers to this question to highlight what is felt to be unsatisfactory about the human condition. Yet for every instance that one might give, counter-examples come to mind. One apparently easy answer might be omniscience. The Jewish God asserts his perfect knowledge extremely early in the Torah, making a tree to instantiate it; and he is not remotely fooled by Adam and Eve's attempts to hide after they have eaten from it. The god of the scientific revolution, the god of Newton, also had perfect knowledge. Despite Newton's heterodox beliefs, his god was still, in one sense, the god of Calvin, who knew the fate of each individual soul just as he foresaw the path of each rolling sphere. But the Greeks, before Plato, allowed for even the king of the gods to be fooled. In the trick at Mekone, Prometheus sacrifices an ox and divides its body parts among two piles, allowing Zeus to choose which will be his portion and which that of Prometheus.

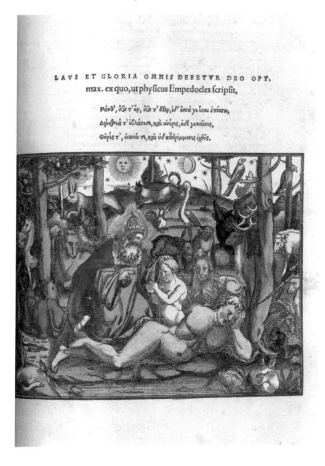

Adam, sleeping here among the beasts in Conrad Gessner's 16th-century *Historia animalium* (History of Animals), had perfect knowledge of God's creation, which early modern naturalists such as John Ray attempted to recover.

John William Waterhouse, *Circe Offering the Cup to Ulysses*, 1891, oil on canvas. Circe successfully attempted to fool the crew of Ulysses, and turned them into animals. However, Ulysses, helped by the advice of Hermes, was able to outwit the Greek goddess in return, and free his crew.

Prometheus carefully hides the good meat under the ox's unappealing stomach, while dressing the bones with shining fat. Zeus falls for the ruse, and selects the bones. It ends badly for Prometheus, but for the rest of humanity, a favourable precedent is set regarding future sacrifices. Hesiod, in his *Theogony*, attempts to salvage Zeus' reputation by having him knowingly tricked; but it is not at all clear that this face-saving gloss was originally present in the tale.

The ancient Greek gods took robust pleasure from their flesh, but human bodies are fated to suffering. Wells's gods, with whom this chapter opened, seem to enjoy freedom from pain and frustration. Similarly, the God of the Quran may send suffering as punishment, or reward those who have undergone suffering for his sake, but does not seem to suffer himself. In this sense, Islam is very different from its parent religions; it is the suffering of Christ that is at the very centre of most versions of Christianity. Indeed, the gods of many other religions have arguments and battles, and are rarely, if ever, described as enduring these without the concomitant feelings that result from them for human beings.

Gods do, perhaps, enjoy more leisure than human beings; their actions are rarely constrained by the need to fulfil the ordinary human conditions of life. There is an existential arbitrariness about the acts they choose to perform. The Sumerian gods, as we have already seen, deliberately created humans as their servants, and almost all of the gods require obeisance from their people in one form or another. Though not obviously making slaves of humans, the Aztec gods did require help from their people in order to do their work – and of a most bloody kind. Without human sacrifice, it was feared that the seasons and the heavens could not be kept on their cycle. Though the Aztecs' sacrifice was not propitiatory in intent, it appears that Spanish Catholicism, with the atoning sacrifice of Christ, was a relatively easy graft onto earlier beliefs.

If there is one quality that pretty much all gods share, it is immortality. Death comes for all humankind; we long to be one of those divine Others for whom it is not so. Those few gods that do die, such as the Norse Baldr or the Christian Jesus, generally resurrect. Strangely enough, the death of an entire pantheon

While many sought the divine and perfection within the spiritual of life, Albrecht Dürer was fascinated by their presence in the physical human form. Adam and Eve were depicted in 1504 based on such a system of measurement and ratios.

seems imaginatively more possible than that of a single god. In Norse mythology, again, this is contemplated in the Ragnarök event, in which the death of the gods plays out alongside the transition of one world-era to the next. For the Aztecs, the commencement of the era of the present Sun was only made possible by the self-sacrifice of many deities.

Few in the West hold out any hope for a god who can save us from death. But there are those who place their faith, or at least hope, in the ability to upload their personalities into the cloud and thereby live eternally. Perhaps, even, their bodies can be saved to last forever, barring accidental defrosting. Before we can

E. Jeaurat's engraving of Vulcan, 1716. Would access to divine artefacts (for example, Jupiter's lightning bolts, Thor's hammer or Vulcan's forge and so on) allow humans to attain divine powers?

This *c.* 10th/11th-century Mayan Rain God was one of the deities that helped in maintaining the cycle of seasons.

understand how and why this notion of immortal apotheosis has come about, we must take a detour via evolution.

The articulation of evolution as the means by which species came into existence is often, naively, identified as the historical moment in which God was extinguished. Theologically speaking, the more interesting corollary of that moment is what it did to humans' understanding of themselves. Having, as they thought, understood the process, they were now in a position to control it. Less than a decade after Darwin published on human evolution, zoologist Edwin Ray Lankester highlighted the need to take control of the process from then on, so as to avoid deterioration of the species. It truly seemed like an opportunity to turbo-charge evolution, to feed the desired results back through the machine of heredity without waiting for the slow selective process of nature. Though there had been no creator at the beginning of the process, humans had now filled the vacancy.

Such optimism resulted in experiments with X-rays and mutagenic chemicals to take crop yield to the next level in plants. In humans, it resulted in a range of interventions under the name of eugenics. Whose values should inform the differential selections and encouragements of the human species? Was there a set of scientifically correct decisions? T. H. Huxley, for all his bullishness about evolution and agnosticism, did not think so. For him, everything that was most civilized and morally upright about humans ran counter to the law of the jungle that ruled

As in this image of human sacrifice from the Aztec *Codex Magliabechiano* (*c.* mid-16th century CE), the immortality of gods was dramatically juxtaposed with the sacrifice of mortal beings. Despite being immortals, the gods still relied on the mortality of human beings.

evolution. Not everyone thought like him, and many scientists became intoxicated by the prospect of ruling the species by defining – racially, medically, tragically – what it meant to be properly 'human'.

Twentieth-century philosophers appropriated the term *Homo faber* – man the maker – to capture the sense that humans, uniquely, are not at the mercy of nature, but can remake it to suit their purposes. In so doing, their name suggests, he has transcended himself to become a new species. *Homo faber* presents us with a double-bind: either he embodies a hubristic segregation of humans from nature (Huxley), or else he causes us to naturalize humanity – for which read 'humans under the law of Darwinian selection' (the eugenists), a contingent, political law of domination by the most powerful.

That dizzy late Victorian excitement about Evolution 2.0 continues to afflict us, like one of those recurring dreams in which we eventually dream-think 'I used to dream about this, and now it's really happening.' It *was* a dream, so the story goes, because the Victorians had no real idea of the science; but today it is 'really' happening because of genetics, or technology, or artificial intelligence – or most likely all three. These factors would lift us from being all-too-human to . . . well, to what, exactly, depends on one's theology: either something better-human, or something beyond-human.

This latest enthusiasm for the god-human – the more-than human – has been building since the 1990s; at this time, feminist scholars even hoped that the military heritage of the robot could be completely repurposed for the coming race – that the new cyborgs would be free from the inheritance of patriarchy and empire. The terms 'transhuman' and 'posthuman' are often used interchangeably for this leap-frog moment, and scholars are beginning to tease apart their many meanings. The conventional distinction is that transhumanism seeks to improve upon the human body, seeking the freedom from suffering that marks out many gods, while posthumanism seeks to move beyond the body altogether, perhaps even to immortality, most especially by taking human existence into the realms of data. At their roots, both trans- and posthumanism are Christo-Platonic, seeking to create humans – or perhaps humanity – cleansed and perfected for the new kingdom.[2] These new philosophies do not merely rehearse earlier iterations of evolutionist fervour; they replicate the very earliest debates of Christianity. Even the body-denying anorexia of some transhumanists echoes the fasting of the Stoics and medieval saints; like the latter, it is not diagnosed as pathological, but gullibly glamorized in the media as a scientific diet to hold off ageing.

Yuval Noah Harari has recently posited a new species – *Homo deus* – that is firmly rooted in this tradition. Humans, he claims, will become gods through biological and technological enhancement, but, above all, through their translation into data. Harari claims to have understood what previous generations have not: that our essence as humans is not the soul, as medieval theology had it; nor free will, as humanism and liberal politics have it; but data processing. Therefore, the rise of intelligent machines, and their imbrication with human existence, are all part of a glorious apotheosis of nature. We, or our technological elite, will become one with the informational flow of the universe. Consciousness is an irrelevance to this process. In its teleological directionality, its cosmic scope and its pivotal role for a technological elite, Harari's vision strongly resembles the millenarianism of the seventeenth and even eighteenth centuries, within whose bounds well-known figures in the history of science laboured piously to bring God's reign into historic reality, through their advances in knowledge.[3] In its vision of disembodied god-humans, it even resembles the medieval picture of the soul. As the philosopher John Gray pithily observes, a writer from a polytheistic tradition would understand something very different by the notion of *Homo deus*.[4] Imagine a Greek pantheon, in which gods quarrel and fight; it is very different from Harari's Platonic 'Dataism'.

'Transhuman' and 'transgender' are terms that speak not only of blurring dualities, but of going above and beyond, in the sense of transcendence. 'Trans' has, arguably, been the defining prefix of the 2010s. Drag artist RuPaul Charles puts his finger on the matter when he discusses the meaning of his TV show *Drag Race*: 'It has politics at its core, because it deals with how do you see yourself on this planet? That's highly political. It's about recognizing that you are God dressing up in humanity.'[5] God dressing up in humanity – it is a brilliant evocation of Christology, and superbly offensive to the straight evangelicalism of his native USA. But for body artists such as Charles, the transhuman is political, perhaps because the supervenience of politics upon the body – particularly the African American, the queer or the feminine body – is so inescapable. The transformations wrought upon the

Transhuman enhancements such as this example of exoskeletal support and movement-generation for a motor-impaired individual seem like a laudable application of science. They seem darker in the context of the Defense Advanced Research Projects Agency's attempts to use them to create externally automated human combatants.

Neil Harbisson self-identifies as a trans-species cyborg: part human, part machine. An antenna implanted in his skull allows him to perceive visible and invisible colours via audible vibrations in his skull as well as to receive information and phone calls directly into his head, via internet connection.

drag body are not ideal or data-Platonic; they are painstaking, uncomfortable and material.

Seeing the body as a political, embodied subject, rather than a modified object, alters the theology of the human. Creating god as Other requires, in the monotheistic faiths, a splitting of the self into the god-compatible part – the soul – and the other Other, the body. Within the logic of these religions, Harari's future selves are our own idols. And what is it, again, that is so wrong about idol-making? Is it, as the monotheistic scriptures state, that humans thereby misdirect their worship to a mute object; or is it the *making itself* that is the problem? The second elevation of Philip, to godhood, undercuts his first elevation, to prince. Post-human idol-makers perhaps demean their own humanity. It may be that the feet of clay are, potentially, the idol-makers' human salvation. As Lytton Strachey observed, 'even clay has a merit of its own; it is the substance of the common earth . . . [bringing the artist] into kinship with the wide humanity of the world.'[6]

6 Alien

In 1905 the artist William Rothenstein produced the striking and disturbing *Aliens at Prayer*. Part of a series of paintings of the East End of London, this showed three Jewish men at synagogue. Contemporary critics chose to interpret it as a technical exercise in working in the style and practice of Old Masters such as Rembrandt. The title, however, suggests that it could just as easily be seen as an overtly political comment on the increasingly unstable situation faced by Jews in Britain.[1] In the same year, after all, the British Parliament had passed the 'Aliens Act'. This, while ostensibly focused on preventing undesirables (paupers, criminals) in general from entering the country, was specifically intended to halt further Jewish immigration from tsarist Russia. Domestic anti-Semitism and fear of economic and social unrest drove the Act, which also had the effect of identifying other groups – Poles, Germans, Chinese – as undesirables, and making their home within the United Kingdom much less secure.[2] Rothenstein's painting encapsulated the familiar, and sometimes fearful, distance often felt when recognizing practitioners of other religions and cultures.

The concept of alienation – of being estranged from that which should be familiar – pervades the Old Testament. The book of Genesis, after all, shows us the first humans alienated from God. Adam and Eve and their children are wrenched from

William
Rothenstein,
Aliens at Prayer,
1905, oil on canvas.

their home and exiled to an environment alien to them. Their descendants – Abraham, Jacob, Joseph, Moses – repeatedly find themselves living as sojourners in foreign lands. The laws laid down by the Pentateuch reflect this – Israel, we are told, must not oppress the alien, but provide justice and protection to it, just as God protected the Israelites when they themselves were alien. Unfortunately, as the British example shows, aliens are far

Raphael, *Ezekiel's Vision*, c. 1518, oil on panel. This vision of God is sometimes interpreted as evidence for biblical extraterrestrials.

more likely to be met with suspicion and hostility, and to be treated in inhumane and dehumanizing ways.

For some, aliens do not even need to be present in order to cast a destabilizing shadow over events, as the infamous picture of a Norwegian bus full of burkha-wearing women showed in

August 2017. The picture, brandished by anti-immigrant groups as proof of the extent of Norway's 'Islamification' was, it transpired, actually a photograph of rows of empty seats.[3] It was a telling demonstration, an inadvertent Rorschach test, of the extent to which the aliens that people see in shadow represent, in fact, their own externalized fear and foreboding. It is also notable that this kind of pareidolia – seeing 'shadow people' where none actually exists – also appears in dealing with other kinds of aliens. We are all familiar with the existence of figures such as the Mars Face or the Man in the Moon, where random forms coalesce into a familiar, if unsettling, pattern. Much more disturbing, however, are the kind of quasi-humanoid shapes seen

Henry Fuseli, *The Nightmare*, 1781, oil on canvas. This is sometimes considered to show the phenomenon of sleep paralysis – one of the explanations offered by sceptics for the experience of alien abduction.

late at night or early in the morning, as people drift off to sleep or rouse to wakefulness. Experienced most frequently by sleep paralysis sufferers, clothes hung on a door, or curtains slung over the back of a chair, can become human-esque entities – sometimes angel, sometimes alien and always unsettling.

Fundamentally then, when it comes to considering the 'human', aliens are the ultimate 'Other', an 'Other' that has always accompanied us. They are the traders, the travellers, the refugees and the honoured guests – as well as the invaders, the colonizers and the undocumented immigrants. We ourselves become alien, as soon as we travel to a place where we are unknown and unknowing. The term has multiple meanings – being a foreigner, being strange or unfamiliar, even being extra-terrestrial (and thus, by definition, not a member of *Homo sapiens*). The potential for slippage between these meanings shows both how ubiquitous and how insidiously dehumanizing the concept can be.

Despite the exhortations of the Old Testament, the human rights of aliens are precarious. After all, by definition, they belong elsewhere, in contrast to 'citizens', who are the legally recognized inhabitants of a nation, state or city, with a legitimate right to live and work in that place. 'Legal' aliens are those non-citizens with permission to be in the country – usually as long as they adhere to a strict set of conditions. 'Illegal' aliens are those without such permission. 'Hostile' aliens, on the other hand, are people who, because of their family background, are potential traitors in time of war – a direct threat to the body politic. Such individuals are liable to summary imprisonment or deportation. German, Austrian and Italian nationals, for example, were interned in their thousands in Britain in the early years of the Second World War, as they were – alongside Japanese civilians – in the United States. The human rights of aliens could thus be revoked at a moment's notice, their movements restricted, their property sequestered, purely on the basis of their place of birth. In the case of George Takei, LGBT activist and *Star Trek* actor, his childhood internment was based on the fact that his grandparents were born in Japan: two generations of American citizenship were insufficient to wipe out the taint of an alien heritage.[4] In other cases, even marriage to an alien could endanger a woman's citizenship: literally, she was sleeping with the enemy, and as such represented a weakness in the nation's security.[5]

In fact, this relationship between aliens, borders and states is as old as nation-states themselves. England, for example, used the 'Alien Act' of 1705, as part of the negotiations surrounding the Act of Union between England and Scotland, to threaten the Scots with an 'alien' status that would entail both loss of property and status. Later, the English Parliament passed the Foreign Protestants Naturalization Act of 1708, to regularize the condition of Huguenot refugees – Protestants fleeing persecution and war on mainland Europe were welcomed by a government concerned that English Catholics were an enemy within, loyal to the pope, rather than to the queen.[6] Nearly a hundred years later, as the spectre of the French Revolution haunted governments on either side of the Atlantic, the United States government passed the 'Alien and Sedition Acts'. These made it harder for an immigrant to become a citizen, and easier for the state to deport or imprison non-citizens. This Act has remained in effect, being used to intern aliens in the World Wars, and was cited during Donald Trump's campaign for the U.S. presidency in support of his plan to ban people from Muslim-majority nations from entering the United States.[7] The existence and deployment of the category of 'alien' remains a key strategy in the management of national security. Fundamentally, aliens may look human, but their access to human rights is revocable. For some, since aliens usually come from a different ethnic background, or follow different faiths, their appearance and actions may mean that – despite being members of *Homo sapiens* – they don't even look human.

In the early twenty-first century the distinction between 'aliens' and 'immigrants' is frequently and visibly elided. 'Illegal' immigrants occupy a profoundly uncertain cultural and legal space, as do – with catastrophic irony – 'indigenous peoples', a phrase often used in the alienation of the first peoples from their own lands. The moral and ethical responsibility of comparatively wealthy individuals and states to support and aid those less fortunate – not least in the name of shared humanity – has run up against fear, suspicion and xenophobia, creating a situation in which even the names applied to people in this position can be problematic. The phrase 'illegal' immigrants, for example, carries deeply troubling implications – how can people be illegal? How can fellow humans be stripped of their humanity in this manner? The u.s. Associated Press and the European Journalism Observatory encourage the use of 'undocumented' or 'unauthorized' instead. But while some media listen, others are less willing to take care.[8]

The trouble is that it is very easy to slide from the notion of alien as 'strange', 'unfamiliar' and 'unknown' to the idea of alien as 'disturbing', as 'threat' and as 'invader' – even when, as with the first peoples, the ostensible alien was actually there first. This slippage is not just facilitated by historical experience, but by broader ecological concerns – look, for example, at the ways in which other kinds of 'aliens' are described. Non-native plants and animals – Japanese knotweed in England, European rabbits in Australia – are frequently vilified and feared because of their vitality and vigour. Often imported from territories conquered by European empire or expropriated from their homelands by imperial representatives in the hope of economic or aesthetic profit, their colonization of unfamiliar environments has been very successful. This overwhelming success has, in turn, led to determined efforts to eradicate them, root, branch and burrow, in the hope of restoring the status quo. There are clear parallels here with the fears that the languages and traditions of local people will be 'swamped' by immigrants who refuse to assimilate. When considering this, also remember that a fundamental aim of imperial Europe was to eradicate indigenous cultures, replacing them with a 'civilization' imposed by soldiers, administrators and politicians. This is beyond irony: it is heartbreakingly unbearable.

While the first peoples were made aliens in their own lands, their freedom to move restricted, their families ripped apart and their languages banned, other humans were literally alienated – stolen, snatched, abducted – from their homes. The lowest

The inhumanity of dealers in human flesh is revealed in this 1892 engraving by Isaac Cruikshank, 'The Abolition of the Slave Trade', in which a fifteen-year-old girl is beaten to death on the deck of a slave-ship.

The ABOLITION of the SLAVE TRADE.
Or the Inhumanity of Dealers in human flesh exemplified in Captⁿ Kimber's treatment of a Young Negro Girl of 15 for her Virgin Modesty

estimates for the number of people forcibly removed from Africa by the Atlantic slave trade stands at around 20 million; equally large numbers are estimated to have been seized for trade around the Indian Ocean and Middle East.[9] These abductions caused unimaginable human misery and suffering; people were abused, treated as chattel, of less value or consequence than domestic animals or equipment.

Any attempt to compare these horrors with the 'alien abduction' phenomenon that swept Western – especially American – cultures in the later twentieth century seems unquestionably offensive. How can there be any comparison between the anguish, death and despair of the slave trade and the – presumably

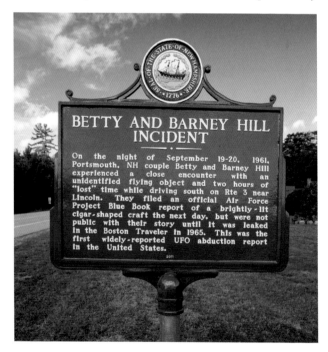

New Hampshire sign memorializing the alien experiences of Betty and Barney Hill. It is another cruel irony that the stories of 'alien' abductees are known so well, while even the names of those abducted into slavery have been eradicated.

imaginary – experiences of (usually) white Americans? But there are unsettling and revealing parallels, with implications that bear closer examination in the context of a sense of historical guilt.

The abduction 'craze' all began in September 1961, on a road through the White Mountains of New Hampshire. Betty and Barney Hill remembered seeing strange lights and shapes in the sky as they drove back home from Canada – but on arrival, they realized that they didn't remember much of the journey itself. Under hypnosis, they recalled being taken aboard an alien ship, where they were separated and subjected to intimate, unwanted and sexualized medical examinations by the aliens.[10] They were by no means the first people to say that they had been abducted by aliens. But the case of the Hills, significantly an interracial couple at a time and in a place where such relationships were regarded with deep suspicion and hostility, brought the subject of alien abduction to the forefront of cultural consciousness, and made it the subject of serious public discussion. In the years that followed, more and more people began to speak about similar memories – often prefaced by the sight of 'shadow people' or even little grey aliens in their bedrooms. Books by figures such as Budd Hopkins, Whitley Strieber, John Mack and David Jacobs became international best-sellers, retelling the stories of apparently astonishing events in a way that made them credible, not least by focusing on the ordinary, everyday nature of the abductees.[11] (Hopkins's suggestion that the then Secretary General of the United Nations – Javier Pérez de Cuéllar – had been abducted in order to prevent him announcing to the world that extra-terrestrials were real may, however, have been a step too far.)[12]

By the mid-1980s UFO abduction was a distinctive cultural phenomenon. Precise numbers of those with memories of abduction were hard to come by – one heavily criticized estimate, based on a 1991 Roper Poll commissioned by abduction researchers, claimed that around 4 million Americans had been affected.[13] Support groups for those who believed they had been abducted appeared, and it even became possible to insure yourself against alien abduction, or any alien pregnancies.[14] In many ways, the experience became almost institutionalized – certainly routinized, with checklists of abduction symptoms – at the same time as critics vigorously contested its reality. Regardless of the 'truth', clearly a significant number of people, who showed no other signs of ill health or instability, held the sincere belief that they had been abducted by extra-terrestrial aliens, who had subjected them to invasive experiments and sexual abuse.

But when considered in the light of debates surrounding race and immigration, the alien abduction phenomenon becomes even more interesting and much more disturbing. In 1997 the film *Men in Black* made this link explicitly. In its initial scenes, law enforcement officials stop a truck that they believe is full of people who are apparently trying to cross the u.s. border illegally. However, one of these hopeful immigrants actually turns out to be Mikey, a grey-skinned reptilian extra-terrestrial hiding behind a fake Hispanic-style head. The film drew on a category of familiar characters from ufo folklore – men, dressed in black suits, who police ufo witnesses, threatening them into keeping quiet about what they have seen. In contemporary folklore, their role is ambiguous – perhaps they work for an unknown, quasi-official agency; perhaps they are even aliens themselves. The 1997 film 'revealed' them to be members of a government organization with responsibility for policing extra-terrestrial movements on Earth. As border agencies do with human migrants, these Men in Black check papers and backgrounds, actively discourage those defined as 'undesirables', make sure that temporary visitors don't outstay their welcomes, and manage their employment and residence status. Aliens, the film indicates, really are among us – they might even be your teachers, your pop stars or your post-office workers.

By definition, aliens come from the other side of a border – whether that be cultural, political, cartographic or interstellar. Their crossings of that border can easily be seen as violations of it: crucially, is it there to mark difference, or as a defence of internal integrity? At the level of the state – or in the case of *Men in Black* or *Independence Day*, the Earth – this is expressed as a threat to national or global security. But individuals also have borders, more commonly understood perhaps as 'personal space' or 'boundaries' – and the narratives of alien abduction clearly focus precisely on the violation of these boundaries. Many abduction stories begin when the individuals are kidnapped from their own

The morally ambiguous Men in Black of UFO folklore police alien residence among unsuspecting human neighbours.

Henrique Alvim Correa's illustration of the 1906 French edition of *War of the Worlds* shows the violence with which H. G. Wells's Martians set about the colonization of England.

homes, in many cases taken against their will from their own bedrooms. The place that should be most private, the safest space, is disrupted by the entry of strangers, intent on forcibly detaining their targets and separating them from their families. Not content with breaching personal and domestic space, these intruders go on to violate individuals' bodily integrity, handling them like animals, probing without permission into the most private of spaces – in fact, acting much as colonial agents did during Europe's encounters with the rest of the world, and as agencies with names like Border Patrol and Border Force continue to do in Western democracies in the present day.

This theme of violation, and its connection to global politics, is key to the science-fiction genre – which, of course, is also based explicitly on engagement with aliens. H. G. Wells's *War of the Worlds*, remember, originated in a nightmarish (for good, middle-class Englishmen, that is) inversion of the colonial experience. As the narrator notes,

> We must remember what ruthless and utter destruction our own species has wrought, not only upon animals . . . but also upon its own inferior [*sic*] races. The Tasmanians, in spite of their human likeness, were entirely swept out of existence in a war of extermination waged by European immigrants, in the space of fifty years. Are we such apostles of mercy as to complain if the Martians warred in the same spirit?[15]

Half a century later, John Wyndham's *Midwich Cuckoos* (1957) showed middle England itself as the target of alien invasion: using rape as a weapon of war, the initial colonizing wave is violently implanted in the wombs of the female victims. The sexual tables were turned even more dramatically in films such as *Species* (1995) and in the *Alien* franchise (1979 onwards). In both these cases, the predatory sexuality at the heart of the horror again involved a profound inversion. The plot of *Alien* was based on the oral penetration of one of the male crew, followed by the use of his body as a gestation chamber for the embryonic Xenomorph. *Species* showed a team of scientists and agents using alien instructions to produce a hybrid being (female, because they assumed that a 'she' would be more docile). Unfortunately, these government-sanctioned Frankensteins soon found themselves – or more specifically, their gonads – targeted by their lethal creation as she sought to harvest their genetic potential for her offspring. When it comes right down to it, aliens are a threat because they are potentially powerful enough to treat white men in the same way that white men have treated people of colour and white women.

Other films made the link between the aliens and the exploitation of different human groups more explicit. *District 9* (2009) showed refugee aliens forcibly restricted to a ghetto settlement outside Johannesburg, using xenophobia and speciesism to explore dehumanizing racism. *Avatar* (2009) evoked memories and experiences of imperialism on a number of levels, but particularly in relation to capitalist hunger for environmental resources. Intriguingly, however, for *Star Wars* and *Star Trek* – two of the most successful science-fiction franchises of all time – aliens mostly are not bad, and baddies mostly are not alien. In other examples of extra-terrestrial contact, humanity's future is not threatened by aliens, but by the fact that governments or corporations consistently fail to act in the best interests of ordinary people. The ambiguity of the 'men in black' is again evoked: are those who exercise power on our behalf themselves fundamentally alienated from 'us'? Neither *ET the Extra Terrestrial* (1983) nor *Close Encounters of the Third Kind* (1977) ever fully explained why aliens had come to Earth, but it was the actions of government agents that actually endangered human lives. In *Contact* (1997), government conspiracy keeps the alien truth hidden, paralleled in *Arrival* (2016), in which military fears and government paranoia prevent effective communication with the aliens. In fact, the concept of 'the government', particularly in Hollywood blockbusters, can be just as alien as the extra-terrestrials – not least because what is often at stake is the fundamental issue of whether you can, in fact, be 'human' if you are not 'humane'. We are left to wonder who 'we' are, if 'they' – our leaders – can act in such inhuman ways: if 'we' are not human to them, are they themselves human?

At the same time, Western culture continues to anticipate the possibilities for eventually communicating with non-human aliens. The idea that the eighteenth-century-born astronomer Johann von Littrow was responsible for the suggestion that a gigantic circular canal should be dug in the Sahara, filled with kerosene and then ignited as a fiery signal of intelligent life on the Earth is almost certainly apocryphal. But certainly, some nineteenth-century astronomers were convinced that they saw evidence of civilization (cities, agriculture, canals) on the Moon, Mars and even Venus; others thought that they had identified signals coming from extra-terrestrial civilizations. So standard was the expectation that Martian life would soon be found that the turn-of-the-century Pierre Guzman Prize, created to reward the first person to communicate with other planets, specifically excluded Mars from the competition. But some sense of how problematic communication with extra-terrestrials would be was found in the difficulties that nineteenth-century scholars had experienced in deciphering Egyptian hieroglyphs. That endeavour had only succeeded through the acquisition of the Rosetta Stone by Western scholars – itself a legacy of Anglo-French imperialism in Egypt, and since 2003 the subject of repatriation requests from the Egyptian state.[16] The stone was inscribed with the same proclamation in three different

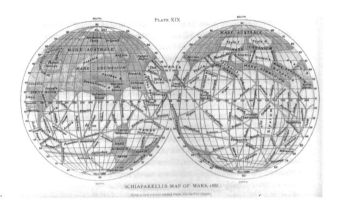

Giovanni Schiaparelli's map of canals on Mars seemed to give evidence of intelligent alien life.

formats: ancient Greek, hieroglyphic script and demotic script. Since Western scholars were familiar with the first of these, they could use the Greek inscriptions in order to decipher the unknown alphabets. But if it was so hard to understand intelligent communications between cultures deeply separated by time, how could communication across space and species be managed?

In the first instance, people turned to invented languages, often using mathematics as a basis. Lancelot Hogben, an eminent British biologist and statistician, gave an address to the British Interplanetary Society, published in 1963, in which he elaborated on his notion of 'Astraglossa'. Slightly tongue-in-cheek, he argued that, if there was such a thing as a field of semantic reference that could be shared by both human and non-human intelligence, it would probably consist, at least in the first instance, of numbers and shapes.[17] Two decades later, Carl Sagan used prime numbers as the basis for his efforts at interstellar communication, and in 2010 Michael Busch developed a binary language that was used in the 'Lone Signal' project to translate and transmit extraterrestrial messages. Notably, Hogben also advised his listeners to turn to prehistoric and protohistoric monuments and scripts

– the Mayan calendar, for example – in order to get a broader sense of how non-Western human cultures had perceived and conceptualized astronomic events, and thus to take the first step towards imagining the alien. But it remains ironic that the medium most often identified as the best way to communicate with aliens – mathematical symbology – is a language that is equally alien to most of the Earth's human population.

Other efforts, however, were more comprehensible – if often more overtly Euro-centric. The *Pioneer* and *Voyager* probes, launched by NASA in the 1970s to explore the solar system and beyond, travelled with plaques and records intended to carry messages from humanity to alien civilizations. Both collections were put together under the supervision of Carl Sagan, with *Pioneer 10* and *Pioneer 11* carrying pictures depicting, among other things, the position of our solar system in relation to the centre of the galaxy, and the position of the Earth within the solar system. It also carried pictures of a naked and obviously Caucasian couple,

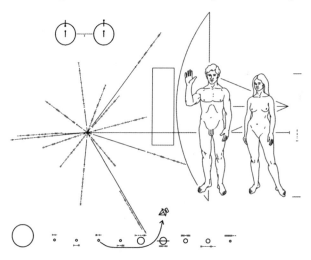

The *Pioneer* plaque, launched into space in the 1970s to announce humanity to alien species.

the man's hand raised in greeting, the woman deferring to him, standing slightly behind and to the side. Perhaps unsurprisingly, while the pictures were controversial, the controversy focused on how explicit the depiction of the woman's vulva should be, rather than on the racist and sexist assumptions contained within the images. The Golden Records sent out on the *Voyager* spacecrafts did, however, contain a greater variety of material, including representations of maths and physics, pictures of animals and plants, and sounds, from Beethoven, Chuck Berry and Kamil Jaliov to whale song and the crash of surf and thunder. These space-based efforts were, of course, made against a wider background of SETI (Search for Extra-terrestrial Intelligence) on the Earth itself, via radio telescope, star surveys and laser-flash searches.

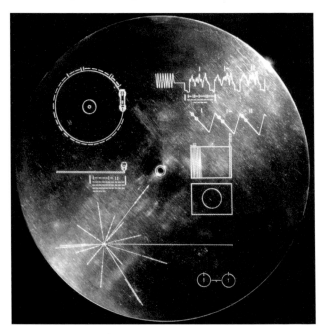

Voyager's Golden Record (1977), featuring the 'Sounds of Earth'.

But are these efforts at communication with aliens actually a good idea? In 2016 the world's largest radio telescope was completed. Built by Chinese scientists in Guizhou Province, it is two-thirds again as big as the u.s.'s Arecibo Observatory, and five times the size of Britain's Jodrell Bank. One of its tasks will be to listen for signs and signals of extra-terrestrial intelligence. One of the honoured guests invited to tour the dish once it was finished was Liu Cixin, author of the global science-fiction best-seller *The Three-Body Problem*, whose work inspired several members of the Chinese Academy of Sciences.[18] It is ironic that Liu's books are actually a bleak Darwinian warning of the dangers of drawing interstellar attention to oneself. In order to survive and grow, Liu argues that all societies must aim to destroy their competitors/neighbours. Successful expansion is only halted when contact is made with a technologically superior civilization – much as with the Middle Kingdom and the arrival of European ships in the nineteenth century. What might, then, be the consequence of modern-world contact with a starfaring alien society? The history of contact between Europeans and Africans, Asians, Australians and indigenous Americans, does not exactly provide a reassuring model.

Fear of being treated by others as you have treated others is an abiding theme when considering the role that the 'alien' plays in drawing human boundaries. People fear that Spanish, or Urdu, will replace English in the shops and streets of Dallas or Manchester, when of course colonized peoples worldwide were forced to learn English to cope in a world run for the benefit of imperial powers. People fear that aliens will abduct them from their homes, remove them from their families, imprison them and subject them to degrading and inhumane treatment – all experiences endured routinely by those suspected of overstaying their visas or of crossing borders 'illegally'. And in both those examples, the noun

The Arecibo message, including information about the structure of human DNA.

'people' mostly refers to white individuals of European descent, who are by no means the only people with a heritage of denying 'humanity' to others, but whose history in that regard is probably the most far-reaching in its global effect.

Finally, it is worth wondering why we are so interested in making contact with extra-terrestrials, when we are so deaf to the sounds of species here on the Earth? Science-fiction author Ted Chiang, working with visual artists Jennifer Allora and Guillermo Calzadilla, pointed out the irony of the Arecibo Observatory in its ecological context – listening intently to the profound silence of space, yet deaf to the cries of the endangered iguaca parrots that inhabit the surrounding forest. Through their film, Chiang, Allora and Calzadilla voice what the iguaca may be saying about the observatory:

I and my fellow parrots are right here. Why aren't they interested in listening to our voices? We're a nonhuman species capable of communicating with them. Aren't we exactly what the humans are looking for? . . .

My species probably won't be here for much longer; it's likely that we'll die before our time and join the Great Silence. But before we go, we are sending a message to humanity. We just hope the telescope at Arecibo will enable them to hear it.

The message is this:

You be good. I love you.

X.[19]

6 Conclusion: Imhumanism

I know that I am a human. But I do not know what a human is.

There is probably very little of which you are more certain than your own humanity, and yet here you are reading a whole book that asks what humans – and implicitly you – are. Indeed, there is a distinct sub-genre of biohistory focused on the exploration of what 'humanity' is, or might be.[1]

Efforts to define humanity – to seek out those characteristics that are uniquely humane – often elide into lists of 'what humans are best at'. Intelligence, manipulation, imagination and the capacity to cooperate (which often involves the creation of stories about self, family, nation or religion) are traits frequently cited in such lists, but do they capture the essence of what it is to be human? The trouble is that as soon as a claim to uniqueness is made, a counter-example can be found. Cooperation? Go to the ant – 'thou sluggard' – and be wise: it has done it far better and longer than we have. Intelligence? Depends on what you mean – you cannot expect a trout to be good at rhetoric, after all – and we would certainly be wise not to forget the potential of artificial life and machine intelligence. Manipulation? The crow, the ape or the rat might give you a run for your money.

What all these definitions offer, however, is an answer to the question 'what am I (a human) like?', rather than to the question 'what is a human?' At their best, such answers may explain species dominance, but they do not identify essence. There are, conceivably, other ways in which a species might dominate the biosphere (telepathy or asexual reproduction, to name two). Why should the question of domination even be answered on the taxonomic level of species? Why not go up to the family level and specify hominins as evolutionary top dogs? Or go down, and nominate a sub-group of humans? Here be the monsters of racial and cultural supremacism – and yet writers on these themes provide no philosophical reason not to make either of these logically equivalent moves. And how to define domination, anyway? Why not give that to ants (so many of them!), or worms (they make the soil that makes the geology) or better yet to *E. coli* (we serve their purposes)? If we were to meet an extraterrestrial top-species, we would not, having read the other books in Reaktion's Animal series, have an answer to the question of how we differ from it.

As soon as we pose the human question historically – *when* did humans come to be? – the concept of humanity evaporates. Pygmy proto-apes – definitely not humans; *Homo sapiens* of today – definitely yes. But what about some in-between hominid 1 million years ago? One hundred thousand years ago? Ninety-nine thousand years ago? The mother of that one? The son? The question of the essence of humanity quickly vanishes into absurdity when pursued with this kind of precision.

Let us ask a different question instead: can a member of *Homo sapiens* fail at being a human? Two major global traditions have veered towards answering this question with a perturbing affirmative. In Confucianism, innate stirrings towards humane action (*ren*, 仁) can be denied, resulting in a less-than-human being. The word 仁 already incorporates the sign for human, so to fail to act humanely is to fail at being human. In Platonism, rationality can fail to manifest, resulting – to speak for a moment in modern mode – in a female, a madman or a bestial being.

The African Roman Terence was commended by Martin Luther for his understanding of the human condition, illustrated here in an edition of his *Comedies* dating from 1150.

The *Oxford English Dictionary* definition of 'human' begins with unintentional ontological astuteness; 'of multiple origins', it notes. Human is a category that has been defined by many things, almost all of them what it is *not*. 'Human' comes from the Greek ὁμός, *homos*, the same; the term only makes sense when we know what is different. The fully human is not the alien, not the machine; not female, not hominin, not animal – although it may perhaps aspire to being God. In almost all cases, this attempt to define the human in contradistinction to another has ended badly. Other beings have been denied personhood; bought, sold, raped and killed. The aim was to define and consolidate humanity, but in the process, the quality of humanity was spent. The human, supposed possessor of humane qualities, lets those very qualities go whenever it tries to assert its humanity.

The human/non-human boundary has in all cases proven difficult to maintain through rationalization of any kind. As soon as a boundary is proposed, counter-examples spring up, whether in philosophy, myth or art. The animal, in many cultures, has a productive and dynamic relation with the human, as guide, as god or as partner. Even in post-Enlightenment societies, we have been repeatedly confronted with the porousness of every boundary (language, rationality) that we have attempted to erect between *Homo sapiens* and other animal species. Machines have come to trouble us with their liveliness; females too have asserted their place within the category of 'us, humans'. Gods of many religions, not least that of Christianity, refuse to be confined to their heavens but intermingle with humans at the deepest level.

One category that we could have investigated in this book, but did not, is that of individuality versus group identity. The sense of the human as, at base, an individual, has been a shibboleth of Western culture over the past two or three hundred years. The human, Euro-Americans insist, is not an ant. In order to retain its humanity, it must fight, in *Star Trek*, the group mind of the Borg; it must fight, in Kafka, the bureaucratic mass. Yet of all the qualities that make *Homo sapiens* unique as an animal (let us forget about the other hominins for a moment), social cooperation is surely pre-eminent. Think – as Sarah Hrdy did, in her book *Mothers and Others* – of a plane journey.[2] Regardless of how cramped, cross or scared we might be, we still manage to get along with the other three hundred strangers on the flight. Replace humans with chimps, Hrdy postulates, and 'any one of us would be lucky to disembark with all ten fingers still attached'. We humans cherish our individuality – but the global success of our species is based on our capacity to act in concert.

The story of humans-as-individuals over the past few hundred years has been bound up with the history of humanism – another mutable term about which a whole different book might be written. What has humanism to do with humans? 'Humanist' denoted, in the sixteenth century, simply a Latin scholar, but in what sense was his work human? In essence, the term referred to the fact that the subject of his (and occasionally her) study was human, rather than divine.

Humanists reanimated respect for classical learning, imbuing antiquity (Plato, Aristotle) with authenticity and truth. At the same time, they encouraged questioning and argument – a critical engagement with textual knowledge. This was a powerful combination of tools, set to work on classical texts newly recovered from the Arab world and new specimens and discoveries from global voyages.

The properties of the world were slowly retrieved from God's hand. European humans increased their sense of agency, both in terms of understanding the world and in being able to control it. No longer were they the passive subjects of God or victims of capricious magic. Words had no power, only things – and things were manipulable by humans (*Homo faber*). Historians have, in recent years, made such simplifications a good deal more complex, but there is still something to them. And as humans became more powerful as subjects, they became more interesting to themselves as subjects. The study of the mind grew as a discipline in its own right: how was it that humans thought, or remembered, or reached legitimate conclusions?

Humanism – unlike the fifteenth-century 'humanist', a person, the term for the philosophy is a nineteenth-century coinage – came to take credit also for the political changes in personhood that occurred during the Enlightenment. Its defining statement might be the affirmation of the Roman playwright Terence: '*Homo sum, humani nihil a me alienum puto*': I am human, and nothing human is alien to me. It was a brave statement from a former slave. For a slave owner to see humanity in his slaves is basic obligation; for a slave to see it in a master is an act of grace. The statement was taken up in the eighteenth century by Alexander Pope, among others, but the tincture of its meaning varied. In some mouths, it could be an assertion of epistemological empire-building:

whatever I see humans do, I can understand and explain it. In others, it could be a statement of moral obligation to act when sympathy with the suffering was engaged. For the founders of the Royal Humane Society, it was both at once. The institution 'for affording immediate relief to persons apparently dead from drowning' was founded by two physicians, and thanks to their tireless campaigning, it acquired royal patronage in about 1787. En passant, it brought the term 'humane' into general use and boasted daughter organizations across Ireland, Europe, America and the West Indies. Both founders, Doctors Hawes and Cogan, were dissenters, and Cogan in particular, though deeply pious, was suspicious of all supernatural doctrine. If hell were real, he once speculated, then 'the propagation of the human species [is] to be placed among the most atrocious of crimes'.[3]

Such a rational approach had to be cautiously wrapped if the Humane Society were to appeal successfully to wealthy donors and supporters. The society carefully positioned itself as performing at once 'the primary and essential duty of Christianity' – that is, of saving lives, or souls – while doing so through rational means.[4] 'It is our happiness to see SCIENCE . . . accomplishing triumphs over the grave,' wrote Hawes, reworking the first letter to the Corinthians. Hawes covered all bases in his appeal to donors, stating that the business of saving lives was a matter of shared humanity with the victim, but glossing this in three different ways: first as fellow citizen and contributor to the economic good of the nation; second, as fellow man, performing a 'labour of love to our fellow creatures'; and third, as fellow Christian, so that no one should die suddenly without the opportunity for penitence. Donors: take your pick. Historians: decide whether the order of given reasons is significant.

At the same time as Hawes was reviving the half-drowned, political writers began to explore the notion of extending full humanity to some unexpected groups, producing tracts such as the *Rights of Man*, or, as Mary Wollstonecraft pointedly corrected Thomas Paine, the *Rights of Woman*. Such texts were taken as foundational in the new French republic and the recently independent United States of America. Needless to say, the extension of humanity was by no means completed even to the rest of *Homo sapiens*. Slavery was practised across Europe and the U.S. for many decades to come, and even after its official cessation racial oppression continues to be systematically manifested.

By the eighteenth or nineteenth century Terence's epithet on humanism could also be taken to mean, in spirit if not in syntax: I am human, and only human things interest me. Marx's philosophy is humanist: the only things that move and change history, in his mind, are the human-made matters of economics. Classic history of science follows in Marx's wake: though the real world is certainly out there, it is only made real to us through the material endeavours of persons. Guns don't kill, so the claim goes; people do.

In recent years, humanism – in both senses of the word – has come under attack. Despite historic assaults on species exceptionalism, it is the rise of the intelligent machine that has – as Lacan described – begun to make humans suspect that they are not the top causal agent in the universe. Instead, machines may have the final say – a concept known as 'the singularity', which has acquired momentum since it was first proposed in the twentieth century. It proposes that a time will come when machines outstrip humans in their computing power, and will begin to procreate by designing their own upgrades and successors. Machines won't, so the story goes, destroy us because they turn evil. We will simply be irrelevant to their continued existence, in just the same way that we bear no particular ill will to orang-utans – we simply desire the palm oil that results in their habitat's destruction. In

John Williamson, *Mary Wollstonecraft*, 1791, oil on canvas. *A Vindication of the Rights of Woman* (1790) largely focused on the need for a rational education for women, and highlighted the roles that educated women played in society.

some respects, this future is already here. International financial dealing is already run by algorithms that are evolving beyond the capacity of humans to understand or control them, seeking gains that threaten all kinds of unpredictable and destabilizing effects on the market (that is, on people) as a whole.

So, do stock market algorithms kill people, or do people?

As we saw in Chapter Five, those who are on the winning side of the current economic system like to believe that they, too, will become posthuman, resurrected with the machines. Margaret Atwood's *MaddAddam* trilogy of novels paints with unforgettable horror the ecological and human flipside of such an arrangement: the ghettoes of the poor and non-posthuman. Suddenly, the hubristic, fallible and partially applied humanism of the eighteenth century does not look so bad in comparison.

Posthumanism also manifests, in fact, not just as an upgrade of the human frame but as a rejection of Enlightenment humanism. As historian John Christie points out, one of the most striking features of Yuval Noah Harari's *Homo Deus* (2015) is its utter lack of hope in humanism or Enlightenment values as the means to hold off the rise of AI and its super-wealthy advocates. Harari accounts for these things as the logical conclusion of the philosophy; humanism, he claims, always contained the seeds of its own destruction, because what counted as the right direction within its schema was simply what made people feel best. Profit and populism were its natural outcomes; there was never any genuine basis for asserting what was *right*. Harari's posthumanism, the triumph of the wealthy cyborgs, is not necessarily likeable, but it is inevitable. It is, once again, Darwin among the machines.

Within the academy, ethically engaged philosophers have attempted to sketch out a less defeatist mode of posthumanist scholarship. Donna Haraway was a pioneer in arguing that animals have more agency than we have recently been inclined to credit them with. Thus humanism, in the sense of human exceptionalism – speciesism, if you will – comes into question. Haraway encourages her readers to understand themselves as radically woven into the fabric of the Earth, to 'inhabit the humusities, not the humanities'.[5] In such accounts, humans can no longer raise themselves above the rest of nature, nor need they abandon themselves to a Darwinian process. Instead, by exploring our knitting-together with the animal world, we can experiment with new ways of re-gathering our relationships with one another and fellow-critters. (Haraway rejects the word 'creatures' as rooted in monotheist theology.) Others, such as Bruno Latour or Jane Bennett, go further, suggesting that even inanimate things are more lively than we give them credit for being. In other words, the humanist dream of being in control of the material world is abandoned; things do have powers, after all. Viruses, to be sure, can have power over us – perhaps so can plastics and pavements and phones.

And yet there is a very significant philosophical problem with posthumanism. We can assert that whales, bacteria, guns and clouds can speak; but we can only hear them do so when they are voiced by humans – returning us to the filter of humanism. Today, that voicing is achieved through a scientific grip on an object – with all the ideological and economic entanglements science brings in its wake.

What we propose as a solution to this paradox might be captured by the term imhumanism. Imhumanism starts from acting *as if* other beings – including humans – are human. Imhumanism takes its name from the theological concept of immanence, and its contrast with transcendence. The immanent god is present within the created world, not beyond it. Indeed, the power of the English language breaks down in the description of an immanent god, for it continues to insist linguistically upon the distinction of the two, the god in the thing, thus replicating Ryle's diagnosis of the category error, the ghost in the machine. True immanence is irreducible to traditional linguistic (that is, subject–object) capture.

Imhumanism, then, holds that humanity is not a quality that can be described or pointed to, either in or beyond the humans that contain it. It is not something that can be searched for in the human as though it were separable from it, or found to be absent in some individuals. Most certainly, it cannot be identified and affirmed in oneself. Nevertheless, humanity is assumed to exist as a quality that simply inheres in the human, and is capable only of being given away, not possessed. It is seen, or rather delineated, in the act of being given away. A quality of being humane is conventionally associated with those who are conferrers of humanity, but this is not the same thing as saying that they are human, or that they have achieved humanity through giving it away. Such a move is invalid within the terms of imhumanism. Only in conferral, a fresh delineation, is humanity made manifest.

One of the most pervasive manifestations of imhumanism occurs in human relations with the dead (remember the Welsh dog's grave from the Introduction?). Almost all cultures grant humanity to those who have died. Evidence of funerary rites is considered to be a quality of humanity in hominins, but from an imhumanist perspective, the point is not to say that this behaviour makes this or that population human. The point is simply to observe the generation of humanity in its conferral to an apparently unlikely other – an unbreathing, even burned, buried or

A lifelike container for the ongoing personhood of Seianti Hanunia Tlesnasa: an Etruscan sarcophagus.

The Day of the Dead in Mexico celebrates the humanity of the deceased, acknowledging their presence among the living.

fleshless corpse. From ancient Egypt to the Día de Muertos in Mexico today, funerals, graves and festivals all assert the right of the dead to be respected and loved, and to remain in human relationship with the living. In not speaking ill of the dead, or abiding as close to that ideal as we can, we extend a level of humane courtesy that is rarely achieved among those still alive. The fates of those who have passed to the next realm are of great concern and interest to us, as is, in some faiths, their new-found ability supernaturally to aid their relatives and acolytes upon the Earth. The dead *are* human, in almost every culture. The horror of the zombie derives not least from the fear that some persons might fail properly to retain this character in their transition to the next world.

Other historically noteworthy examples of imhumanism at work include the conferral of humanity upon slaves, children and women. This is *not* to argue that non-males, non-whites and so on

Josiah Wedgwood's successful anti-slavery medallion of 1787 appealed for the granting of humanity to slaves.

were not human until enlightened white males kindly told them that they could be. Quite the reverse. If anything, we argue that, once oppressors become aware of their misjudged exclusive claim to humanity, they themselves could not be fully human until they had put things right. This perspective resonates with Frantz Fanon's efforts to develop a post-colonial humanism rooted in a recognition that colonialism damages the colonizer as much as it torments the colonized.[6] Yet compassion (whether overdue or spontaneous) does not purchase humanity for its practitioner. Such a calculus runs the risk of slipping back into the question 'is x human?', which is precisely the question that, as we have

MONKEYANA.

AM. I
A
MAN AND
A
BROTHER?

AM I satyr or man ?
Pray tell me who can,
And settle my place in the scale.
A man in ape's shape,
An anthropoid ape,

An offensive
post-Darwinian
reworking of
Wedgwood's
Man and Brother
deliberately
muddled Black
people and apes.

repeatedly observed, dehumanizes us. Meanwhile, one must observe that those not on the top of the cultural heap have created, and continue to use, their own hierarchies. Even the oppressed have the same inclination to find an Other against which to measure their own humanity, whether that Other is their oppressor or somebody else. Nobody has a stronger claim than anyone else to humanity. Imhumanism does not attribute humanity but is about the *act* of attribution.

Human beings have wrestled with opportunities for giving humanity away in the past, and continue to do so in respect of new opportunities that appear in the present. The potential personhood of animals is one example that has stimulated urgent thought and action in both past and present. By the end of the nineteenth century, the term 'humane' had, in ordinary language, been reduced to something like 'kind-hearted', and was particularly widely used in relation to the many organizations then springing up against vivisection and the feather trade. In other

Pareidolia is the widespread human tendency to perceive or attribute humanity where there are only approximate shapes of facial features present. The Man in the Moon is one of the most famous examples.

Giuseppe Arcimboldo's *The Jurist*, 1566, oil on canvas, seems to do the opposite of pareidolia; what appears to be a face is in fact an unpleasant concoction of flesh and fish. Other of Arcimboldo's portraits, made of fruit, flowers and vegetables, are less contemptuous towards their subjects.

words, being humane was a quality directed towards animals. Dismissed at the time as the attribute of silly ladies or loveless old spinsters (note the gender specificity here), this quality of the humane has had a renaissance in recent science.

Anthropology has highlighted, for those of us that no longer live in such societies, that traditional hunting communities tend to regard the animals that they kill as non-human persons. These

FIRST STAGE OF CRUELTY.

animistic people see the world in terms of who, not what. Odd as this might seem, anthropologists have come to a positive view of such ontologies as productive and sustainable ways of living in the world, in both practical and spiritual terms.[7] And of course, even within the West, many of those who keep pets treat them as people, while most of those who work daily with large mammals (horses, cows, pigs) take their individuality and their personality as a matter of course. If you want your day to run smoothly, it matters which cow has a mean streak and which horse is scared of metal gates. Meanwhile, the psychologist Emma Alleyne has made cruelty to animals and its relationship to inter-human psychology the topic of her research career to date. Childhood animal abuse is an extremely strong and well-attested predictor of adult human violence. Thus, as Alleyne notes, 'although the question of cause and effect remains unresolved, it is . . . clear that people who perpetrate animal abuse are cause for concern for wider society because they are likely to engage in other crimes such as property damage, theft, and even interpersonal violence.'[8] Ongoing research attempts to uncover the intrinsic and social factors that produce childhood animal abuse, why it assumes different levels of severity, and how it is channelled in adulthood. Giving our humanity away to animals is something that already happens, for good or ill.

Can we go further? What about insects, bacteria, mosses, or even lakes or rivers?

In 1972 the legal scholar Christopher Stone wrote a revolutionary article entitled 'Should Trees Have Standing?', in which he presented the notion of legal rights for non-human beings, or, in his words, 'the argument for "personifying" the environment'.[9] Philosophically, he points out that many inanimate things have standing – that is, personhood – in law, such as trusts and corporations. Moreover, he alerts us to the realization that even apparent 'people' are, in law, sometimes only constructions; this was the problem of medieval scholars, seeking to understand how the king's word could stand in law even after the king himself had died. Humanity, in a legal sense, was extended beyond the grave, or conferred upon a representative entity.

Stone makes an imhumanist move when he compares the imaginative difficulty in extending standing to trees with past travails in doing the same for minority groups and women in the U.S. It is, above all, a question of the enlargement of empathy through the recognition of difference:

To be able to get away from the view that Nature is a collection of useful senseless objects is . . . deeply involved in the development of our abilities to love – or, if that is putting it too strongly, to be able to reach a heightened awareness of our own, and others' capacities in their mutual interplay. To do so, we have to give up some psychic investment in our sense of separateness and specialness in the universe.

Stone points out, as Latour was to do again a generation later, that there is always a chicken-and-egg problem when it comes to extending rights to entities not considered fully human:

there will be resistance to giving the thing 'rights' until it can be seen and valued for itself; yet, it is hard to see it and value it for itself until we can bring ourselves to give

it 'rights' – which is almost inevitably going to sound inconceivable to a large group of people.[10]

In 2017 something as inconceivable as Stone imagined actually came to pass. A Māori tribe of North Island, New Zealand, succeeded in having the Whanganui River, which they regard as their ancestor, written into law as a living entity with legal status – in ordinary parlance, a person. The move was not without resistance. On the website of *The Guardian*, a liberal newspaper, the story generated a higher than usual quantity of offensive comments. Many respondents were deeply troubled and provoked by this extension of humanity. Among those posts that were left undeleted by the moderators, the leading focus for derision was the observation that a river cannot make use of many legal rights enjoyed by humans, such as education; and that it is not a full legal person unless it can also be held responsible for its

John Singleton Copley, *The Return of Neptune*, c. 1754, oil on canvas. While giving legal status to natural entities seems like an unusual act, elements of nature have traditionally been associated with divine beings who were often represented in human forms. For example, Neptune was the god of the sea in ancient Roman religion.

misdeeds, such as flooding. But as Stone himself points out, not all laws pertain to all people. Laws of the road do not give children the right to drive. People in prison – in the UK, as in many countries – do not have the right to vote. And so on. On the point of responsibilities, Stone suggests that trust funds might be established for natural entities under the care of a guardian, in which case such funds could, in future, also be used to pay out in the case of natural disasters. Altogether, the rights of persons – whether humanoid or not – are neither absolute nor inalienable, but graduated and negotiable.

Foetuses are an especially difficult case for the imhumanist. Here, the hard-won humanity of female persons seems to be in conflict with the potential humanity of the foetus, a zero-sum game. To put the paradox another way, the tribe that fights so hard to deny women full personhood appears to be in the vanguard of imhumanism for another entity – the foetus. This case, however, highlights that the conferral of humanity is not a virtue-machine or a humanity-making device for the donor; that is, it is by no means automatic that one becomes more fully human by giving away humanity. To attempt to assert this as a law once again infracts against the key claim of imhumanism – that humanity can only ever be conferred, not grasped. Some women, in some pregnancies, may confer personhood upon a foetus. But this does not make those women better or more fully human people. In another politics, perhaps foetuses *will* be granted personhood. But in this other politics, both 'women' and 'foetuses' will be differently constituted – along with many other things.

Can we go further still? What about machines? Why do pandas and perhaps even forests seem like legitimate recipients of personhood but not inanimate objects, at least to the authors of this book? Can we grant non-human person status to machines without accepting the corollary that humans are elevated to

Carl Fredrik Reuterswärd, *Non-Violence*, 1985. Is it guns or humans that kill? This sculpture leaves the answer ambiguous: a human condition is embodied by a mechanical artefact.

Creator status, or without creating a flat ontology, an ultra-Darwinian world wherein everything is of equal value?

Perhaps it is most productive to realize that we have already conferred humanity upon inanimate objects. What, after all, do archivists do but grant personhood to pieces of paper? And now they do the same for electronic archives and voices, speaking *things*. As Chapter Three explored, humans have, for a very long time, personified machines, sometimes productively and sometimes with a view to protecting exclusivity for certain classes of human. The challenge is to see and judge what political forms of human being are delineated by the automaton, or by AI.

So what is it to be human? This book has explored the ways in which key cultural categories – beast, hominin, machine, female, god, alien – have been used as a border between humans and Others, with consequences that are frequently frustrating, often tragic, sometimes unendurable. Pets and porpoises can be persons – but this is not a privilege extended to every member of our species. Fear, selfishness, ignorance and sheer self-preservation in the

The short-lived TV series *Me and the Chimp* (1972) presented Buttons the chimp as part of the family, thereby not only considering Buttons as a companion species, but integrating the chimp into the American family unit. What Buttons thought about this, given the suffering endured by animals utilized by the film industry, is less clear.

face of the unfamiliar have all been factors in selectively withholding 'human' status. What is ironic, of course, is that throughout the course of human history, progress, creativity, innovation, inspiration – even, perhaps, humanity itself – have all emerged from contact between peoples and cultures. These contacts have not always been peaceful – but inherent in them has been the acknowledgement of some element of the familiar in the strange, an act of imhumanism that does not define the human, but celebrates shared humanity. That recognition is not necessarily species-bound – and yet as such, in the Anthropocene, it may represent one of the few tools we have to save *Homo sapiens*.

Timeline of the Human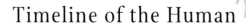

10–4 MYA (MILLION YEARS AGO)	3.6 MYA	2.6 MYA	300–200 KYA (THOUSAND YEARS AGO)
The last common ancestor that humans have with the other great apes lives	Footprints, preserved in volcanic ash in Laetoli, East Africa, provide the first evidence of hominin bipedalism	Stone implements from this date found at Olduvai Gorge, Tanzania, show that hominins had begun to use tools at this time	Anatomically modern human beings appear: Mitochondrial Eve probably lived

8–5 KYA	3 KYA	C. 600–500 BCE	500 BCE	300 BCE
Cities, pottery, smelting and alcohol develop in the Middle East	Invention of writing and paper (Egypt)	Major religions develop: Krishna tradition established; Torah compiled; Zoroastrianism flourishes; Confucian writings emerge; Buddha is born	Invention of the stirrup (India)	The blast furnace enables manufacture of cast iron (China)

1804	1859	1899	1948
Global population of humans is estimated to have reached 1 billion. The next billion took over a century (1927); the one after, a third of that	Humans are displaced from the centre of the animal kingdom by Darwin's *On the Origin of Species*	Humans are displaced from mastery of the conscious mind by Freud's *Interpretation of Dreams*.	The United Nations' Universal Declaration of Human Rights is published

70 KYA	50 KYA	10 KYA
Homo sapiens migrates out of Africa	Evidence of behavioural modernity, such as burial, cave paintings and a more complex set of tool technology	The 'Neolithic Revolution' occurs – humans move from hunting and gathering to settled agriculture

LATE 1300S	1492	1543	1770	C. 18TH CENTURY
Development of the first hand-held, smooth-bore, projectile weapons (Europe)	Bacteria and viruses causing disease in Europeans are introduced to South America	Humans displaced from centre of cosmos by Copernicus' *De revolutionibus*	Coal-fired engines are developed, commencing dramatic atmospheric-carbon growth	Philosophies of human dignity and rights are developed; the concepts of capitalism and free markets are articulated (Europe)

1969	1976	2016	2050
Humanity reaches the Moon	The role of human-made chemicals in ozone layer depletion is established. By 2003 depletion was shown to have slowed thanks to global control of CFCs	The warmest year on record to date. Geologists argue that the Earth has entered a new geological age – the Anthropocene – marked by human impact	Carbon output must hit net zero, according to IPCC report of 2018; there is a one in twenty chance of human extinction having occurred

References

INTRODUCTION: *HOMO SAPIENS*

1 Global Mammal Assessment Team 2008, '*Homo sapiens*', www.iucnredlist.org, accessed 2 April 2019.
2 Arthur Keith, *The Construction of Man's Family Tree* (London, 1934).
3 Milford H. Wolpoff, John Hawks and Rachel Caspari, 'Multiregional, Not Multiple Origins', *American Journal of Physical Anthropology*, cxii/1 (2000), pp. 129–36.
4 Chris Stringer, 'Out of Ethiopia', *Nature*, cdxxiii/6941 (June 2003), pp. 693–5.
5 Chris Clarkson et al., 'Human Occupation of Northern Australia by 65,000 years ago', *Nature*, dxlvii/7663 (July 2017), pp. 306–10.
6 Maanasa Raghavan et al., 'Genomic Evidence for the Pleistocene and Recent Population History of Native Americans', *Science*, cccxlix/6250 (August 2015), p. 841; Pontus Skoglund et al., 'Genetic Evidence for Two Founding Populations of the Americas', *Nature*, dxxv (September 2015), pp. 104–8.
7 Derek Wildman et al., 'Implications of Natural Selection in Shaping 99.4% of Nonsynonymous dna Identity Between Humans and Chimpanzees: Enlarging Genus *Homo*', *pnas*, c/12 (June 2003), pp. 7181–8.
8 J. F. O'Connell, K. Hawkes and N. G. Blurton Jones, 'Grandmothering and the Evolution of *Homo erectus*', *Journal of Human Evolution*, xxxvi/3–4 (1999), pp. 461–85.
9 Andrew Curry, 'The Milk Revolution', *Nature*, d/7460 (August 2013), pp. 20–22. But note also J.B.S. Haldane, *Daedalus; or, Science*

and the Future (London, 1924), on the indecency of drinking the secretions of a cow.

10 Guy Winch, 'Why We Need to Take Pet Loss Seriously', www.scientificamerican.com (May 2018).

11 Adam Taylor, 'Why the Language We Use to Talk About Refugees Matters So Much', www.washingtonpost.com (30 July 2015).

12 G. Agamben, *The Open: Man and Animal* (Stanford, CA, 2004), pp. 33–8.

1 BEAST

1 Douglas Adams, *The Hitchhiker's Guide to the Galaxy* (London, 1979), p. 119.

2 *Taoist teachings from the book of Lieh Tzŭ*, www.wikisource.org, accessed 4 April 2019.

3 John Locke, *An Essay Concerning Human Understanding* (1689), www.earlymoderntext.com, accessed 4 April 2019.

4 Irene Pepperberg, *The Alex Studies: Cognitive and Communicative Abilities of Grey Parrots* (Cambridge MA, 1999).

5 Paul Cobley et al., eds, *Semiotics Continues to Astonish: Thomas A. Sebeok and the Doctrine of Signs* (Boston, MA, 2011), ch. 1, 'Thomas A. Sebeok: Biography and 20th Century Role', pp. 1–18, esp. p. 5.

6 Malcolm Bull, *The Mirror of the Gods: How Renaissance Artists Rediscovered the Pagan Gods* (Oxford, 2005), p. 167.

7 S. K. Robisch, *Wolves and the Wolf Myth in American Literature* (Reno, NV, 2009).

8 Panda Pause, Episode 102, www.stitcher.com, accessed 4 April 2019.

9 Selwyn Brinton, *The Renaissance in Italian Art (Sculpture and Painting): Padua, Verona, Ferrara, Parma, Venice* (London, 1898), p. 120.

10 Sharon E. Roberts et al., 'Clinical Interaction with Anthropomorphic Phenomenon: Notes for Health Professionals about Interacting with Clients Who Possess This Unusual Identity', *Health and Social Work*, XL/2 (2015), pp. e42–e50.

11 Ibid.

2 HOMININ

1 Matthew Eddy, 'The Prehistoric Mind as a Historical Artefact', *Notes and Records of the Royal Society*, LXV/1 (2011), pp. 1–8.
2 John Frere, 'Account of Flint Weapons Discovered at Hoxne in Suffolk', *Archeaologica*, XII (1800), pp. 204–5; Marianne Sommer, *Bones and Ochre: The Curious Afterlife of the Red Lady of Paviland* (Cambridge, MA, 2008), pp. 52–3.
3 J. Prestwich, 'On the Occurrence of Flint-implements, Associated with the Remains of Extinct Mammalia, in Undisturbed Beds of a Late Geological Period', *Proceedings of the Royal Society of London*, X (1859), pp. 50–59.
4 Arthur Keith, *Ancient Types of Man* (London, 1911); Louis Leakey, *Adam's Ancestors: An Up-to-date Outline of What Is Known About the Origin of Man* (London, 1934); Amanda Rees, 'Stories of Stones and Bones: Disciplinarity, Narrative and Practice in British Popular Prehistory, 1911–1935', *British Journal for the History of Science*, XLIX/3 (2016), pp. 433–51. For the cricket bat, see Robin McKie, 'Piltdown Man: British Archaeology's Greatest Hoax', www.theguardian.com (4 February 2012).
5 Johannes Krause et al., 'The Complete Mitochondrial DNA Genome of an Unknown Hominin from Southern Siberia', *Nature*, CDLIV (April 2010), pp. 894–7; Richard Green et al., 'A Draft Sequence of the Neanderthal Genome', *Science*, CCCXXVIII (May 2010), pp. 710–22.
6 Paige Madison, 'The Most Brutal of Human Skulls: Measuring and Knowing the First Neanderthal', *British Journal for the History of Science*, XLIX/3 (2016), pp. 411–32.
7 Michael Hammond, 'Expulsion of Neanderthals from Human Ancestry: Marcellin Boule and the Social Context of Scientific Research', *Social Studies of Science*, XII/1 (1982), pp. 1–36.
8 H. G. Wells, *The Grisly Folk, and the Wild Asses of the Devil* (Gloucester, repr. 2016), originally published in *Storyteller Magazine* (April 1921).

9   H. J. Fleure and T. C. James, 'Geographical Distribution of Anthropological Types in Wales', *Journal of the Royal Anthropological Institute*, XLVI (January–June 1916), pp. 35–153.

10 William L. Straus and A.J.E. Cave, 'Pathology and the Posture of Neanderthal Man', *Quarterly Review of Biology*, XXXII/4 (1957), pp. 348–63.

11 Jean M. Auel, *Clan of the Cave Bear* (New York, 1980).

12 Penny Spikins et al., 'From Homininity to Humanity: Compassion from the Earliest Archaics to Modern Humans', *Time and Mind*, III/3 (2010), pp. 303–25.

13 Katerina Harvati et al., 'Neanderthal Taxonomy Reconsidered: Implications of 3D Primate Models of Intra- and Interspecific Differences', *PNAS*, CI/5 (2004), pp. 1147–52.

14 Roy Lewis, *What We Did To Father* (London, 1960).

15 UN Security Council, 'Resolution 1820 on Women, Peace and Security', www.unwomen.org (2008).

16 This may, as Björn Kurtén's novel *Dance of the Tiger* (New York, 1980) suggests, explain Neanderthal extinction via a combination of hyper-stimulated neoteny and hybrid sterility.

17 See P. Spikins et al., 'Living to Fight Another Day: The Ecological and Evolutionary Significance of Neanderthal Healthcare', *Quaternary Science Reviews* (2018).

3 MACHINE

1   The tale is recounted in the *Liezi* (attributed 5th century BCE, compiled 4th century CE). Available as *Taoist Teachings from the Book of Lieh-Tzŭ*, trans. Lionel Giles (1912) at https://en.wikisource.org.

2   Vera Keller, 'Drebbel's Living Instruments, Hartmann's Microcosm, and Libavius's Thelesmos: Epistemic Machines before Descartes', *History of Science*, XLVIII/1 (2010), pp. 39–74.

3   Cressy Dymock, *An Invention of Engines of Motion Lately Brought to Perfection* (London, 1651), p. 1. Dymock did not mean the same thing as is meant today by perpetual motion; for him and his early modern contemporaries, it was a synonym for the *primum mobile*.

4 Simon Schaffer, 'Machine Philosophy: Demonstration Devices in Georgian Mechanics', *Osiris*, IX (1994), pp. 157–82.

5 Something like a Newton's cradle, as it is now known, was actually described and drawn by Edme Mariotte. See Rod Cross, 'Edme Mariotte and Newton's Cradle', *Physics Teacher*, L/4 (2012), pp. 206–7.

6 Simon Schaffer, 'The Show that Never Ends: Perpetual Motion in the Early Eighteenth Century', *British Journal for the History of Science*, XXVIII/2 (1995), pp. 157–89.

7 Siri does have several different 'default' voices, depending on location, and it is possible for the operator to choose a male version.

8 Jean-Joseph Goux, 'Lacan Iconoclast', in *Lacan and the Human Sciences,* ed. Alexandre Leupin (Lincoln, NB, 1991), pp. 109–22.

9 'Handsets Get Taken to the Grave', BBC News, 29 March 2006, www.bbc.co.uk/news.

10 Repr. in Thomas Watson and Samuel Lee, *The Bible and the Closet; or, How We May Read the Scriptures with the Most Spiritual Profit* (Boston, MA, 1842), p. 55.

11 Marianne Winder, 'Aspects of the History of the Prayer Wheel' (1992), unpublished MS at www.repository.cam.ac.uk.

12 Lynn Townsend White, *Medieval Technology and Social Change* (Oxford, 1962), p. 86. In Arthur C. Clarke's story 'The Nine Billion Names of God' (1953), a similar mechanical process culminates in the death of the universe.

13 Deb Platt, 'Click Here for Good Karma', 1996, www.whatdoyouthinkmyfriend.com, accessed 8 October 2019.

14 George Berkeley, *A Treatise Concerning the Principles of Human Knowledge* (Dublin, 1710), Principle 145.

15 'Passing', originally used in the U.S. to indicate African Americans' acceptance as 'white', is now often used in relation to matters of trans-genderism. Here we stretch the word further to sexuality in order to make a point, but not, I think, beyond the general public's smearing of issues to do with gender and sexuality (implicit, for example, in the category-mixing term LGBT).

4 SHE

1 Appearing first as a serial in the British magazine *The Graphic* during the winter of 1886–7, *She: A History of Adventure* was published as a book by Longmans of London later in 1887.

2 Ayesha does not crumble away permanently, however. In the next book in the series, *Ayesha: The Return of She* (London, 1905), Leo and Holly visit Tibet, where they find a reincarnation of Ayesha ruling another lost kingdom, an encounter that, unfortunately, proves fatal for Leo.

3 C. S. Lewis, *The Magician's Nephew* (Oxford, 1955).

4 Joan Aiken, *The Stolen Lake* (London, 1981). The phrase 'Rex quondam, rexque futurus', or the 'Once and Future King' was allegedly carved on Arthur's tomb at Glastonbury, according to Sir Thomas Malory's *Le Morte d'Arthur*.

5 Originally a play, and then a British TV series also shown on the American PBS Network, *Rumpole of the Bailey* (London, 1978) also became a book and radio series. The books remain in print, and the most recent instalments in the radio series were broadcast on the BBC's Radio 4 station in Spring 2018.

6 Judith Bourne, *The First Women Lawyers in Great Britain and the Empire Record* (London, 2016).

7 *Frasier* was broadcast on the NBC network in the U.S. from 1993 to 2004; *Dad's Army* was broadcast on the BBC in Britain from 1968 to 1977. Both programmes achieved global audiences and are still re-run worldwide.

8 *The Big Bang Theory* premiered on the American CBS network in 2007. It completed its twelfth and final season in 2019.

9 William Blackstone, *Commentaries on the Laws of England*, vol. I (London, 1765), pp. 442–5.

10 Charles Dickens, *Oliver Twist* (London, 1838).

11 Sarah Pomeroy, *Goddesses, Whores, Wives and Slaves: Women in Classical Antiquity* (London, 1994).

12 Katie Pickles, 'Why New Zealand Was the First Country Where Women Won the Right to Vote', www.theconversation.com

(September 2018); Sheila Perry, ed., *Aspects of Contemporary France* (London, 1997); Helen Pankhurst, *Deeds Not Words: The Story of Women's Rights, Then and Now* (London, 2018).

13 This phrase has also been applied to other powerful political women, including Gandhi, Thatcher, Kenya's Amina Mohammed, Sri Lanka's Sirimavo Bandaranaike and Jayaram Jayalalithaa of India.

14 D. H. Lawrence, *Assorted Articles* (London, 1929), quoted in Letty M. Russell, *Human Liberation in a Feminist Perspective* (Philadelphia, PA, 1974), p. 148.

15 Dorothy Sayers, *Unpopular Opinions* (London, 1946).

16 See, for example, John Gray's very lucrative *Men are from Mars, Women are from Venus* (New York, 1992) series.

17 Thomas Laqueur, *Making Sex: Body and Gender from the Greeks to Freud* (Cambridge, MA, 1994), pp. 26 and 28.

18 Michel de Montaigne, *Essays*, Book 1, ch. 20, 'Of the Force of Imagination', www.gutenberg.org, accessed 3 April 2019.

19 Helen O'Connell, Kalavampara Sanjeevan and John Hutson, 'Anatomy of the Clitoris', *Journal of Urology*, CLXXIV/4 (October 2005), pp. 1189–95. Federico Andahazi's *The Anatomist* (New York, 1999) provides a fictionalized account of Columbus' 'discovery' and its political and intellectual impact.

20 There is, however, considerable debate about when and why this happened. See Helen King, *The One-sex Body on Trial* (Abingdon, 2014); Thomas Laqueur, 'Sex in the Flesh', *Isis*, XCIV/2 (June 2003), pp. 300–306; Michael Stolberg, 'A Woman Down to Her Bones: The Anatomy of Sexual Difference in the Sixteenth and Early Seventeenth Centuries', *Isis*, XCIV/2 (June 2003), pp. 274–99; Londa Schiebinger, 'Skelettestreit', *Isis*, XCIV/2 (June 2003), pp. 307–31.

21 Londa Schiebinger, 'Skeletons in the Closet: The First Illustrations of the Female Skeleton in Nineteenth Century Anatomy', in *Feminism and the Body*, ed. Londa Schiebinger (New York, 2000); Londa Schiebinger, *The Mind Has No Sex? Women in the Origins of Modern Science* (Cambridge, MA, 1991); Eric Plemons ,'Description of Sex Difference as Prescription for Sex Change: On the Origins of

.Facial Feminisation Surgery', *Social Studies of Science*, XLIV/5 (May 2014), pp. 657–79.

22 Susan Mosedale, 'Science Corrupted: Victorian Biologists Consider "The Woman Question"', *Journal of the History of Biology*, XI/1 (Spring 1978), pp. 1–55.

23 Nathan Q. Ha, 'The Riddle of Sex: Biological Theories of Sex Difference in the Early Twentieth Century', *Journal of the History of Biology*, XLIV/3 (2011), pp. 505–46.

24 Sarah Richardson, *Sex Itself: The Search for Male and Female in the Human Genome* (Chicago, IL, 2014); Anne Fausto-Sterling, *Sexing the Body: Gender Politics and the Construction of Sexuality* (New York, 2000); Stephen Brush, 'Nettie M Stevens and the Discovery of Sex Determination by Chromosomes', *Isis*, LXIX/2 (June 1978), pp. 163–72; Chandak Sengoopta, *The Most Secret Quintessence of Life: Sex, Glands and Hormones, 1850–1950* (Chicago, IL, 2006); Nelly Oudshoorn, *Beyond the Natural Body: An Archaeology of Sex Hormones* (London, 1994).

25 Emily Martin, 'The Egg and the Sperm: How Science Has Constructed a Romance Based on Stereotypical Male–Female Roles', *Signs*, XVI/3 (Spring 1991), pp. 485–501; Gerald Schatten and Heide Schatten, 'The Energetic Egg', *The Sciences*, XXIII/5 (September–October 1983), pp. 28–35.

26 John Money and Anke Ehrhardt, *Man and Woman, Boy and Girl* (Baltimore, MD, 1972); Marianne van den Wijngaard, 'Feminism and the Biological Construction of Female and Male Behaviour', *Journal of the History of Biology*, XXVII/1 (Spring 1994), pp. 61–90.

27 Edward Wilson, *Sociobiology: A New Synthesis* (Cambridge, MA, 1975); Richard Dawkins, *The Selfish Gene* (Oxford, 1976); Ullica Segerstrale, *Defenders of the Truth: The Battle for Science in the Sociobiology Debate and Beyond* (Oxford, 2000).

28 Robert Trivers, 'Parent Investment and Sexual Selection', in *Sexual Selection and the Descent of Man*, ed. B. Campbell (Chicago, IL, 1972), pp. 136–79.

29 Jeff Guo, 'Researchers Have Found a Major Problem with "The Little Mermaid" and Other Disney Movies', www.washingtonpost.

com (25 January 2016); 'An App to Help You Speak Up', BBC News, www.bbc.co.uk (6 October 2017).

30 Marianna Torgovnick, *Gone Primitive: Savage Intellects, Modern Lives* (Chicago, IL, 1990), pp. 42–72.

5 GOD

1 Gananath Obeyesekere, *The Apotheosis of Captain Cook: European Mythmaking in the Pacific* (Princeton, NJ, 1992); Marshall Sahlins, *Islands of History* (Chicago, IL, 1985, repr. 2013).

2 Meghan O'Gieblyn, 'Ghost in the Cloud: Transhumanism's Simulation Theology', *n+1* (Spring 2017), www.nplusonemag.com.

3 Charles Webster, *The Great Instauration: Science, Medicine and Reform, 1626–1660* (London, 2002), pp. 2 and 9.

4 John Gray, 'Humanity Mk II: Why the Future of Humanity Will Be Just as Purposeless as the Past', *New Statesman* (13 October 2016), www.newstatesman.com.

5 Decca Aitkenhead, 'RuPaul: "Drag is a Big F-you to Male-dominated Culture"', *The Guardian* (2 March 2018), www.theguardian.com.

6 Lytton Strachey, *Landmarks in French Literature* (London, 1912), p. 79.

6 ALIEN

1 Samuel Shaw, 'Rembrandt and Reality', in *In Focus: The Doll's House 1899–1900 by William Rothenstein*, ed. Samuel Shaw (London, 2016), available at www.tate.org.uk.

2 Jill Pellew, 'The Home Office and the Aliens Act, 1905', *Historical Journal*, XXXII/2 (June 1989), pp. 369–85.

3 Jon Henley, 'Bus Seats Mistaken for Burquas by Members of Anti-immigrant Group', *The Guardian* (2 August 2017), www.theguardian.com.

4 George Takei, 'At Least During the Internment . . . Words I Never Thought I'd Utter', *Foreign Policy* (18 June 2018), www.foreignpolicy.com.

5 See, for example, the British Nationality and Status of Aliens Act 1914, www.legislation.gov.uk, accessed April 2019 – although in wartime, a woman married to an alien could apply to resume her British nationality.

6 Stephen Conway, 'Christians, Catholics, Protestants: The Religious Links of Britain and Ireland with Continental Europe, *c.* 1689–1800', *English Historical Review*, cxxiv/509 (August 2009), pp. 833–62.

7 Duncan Williams and Gideon Yaffe, 'Trump's Administration Says the Travel Ban Isn't Like Japanese Internment. It Is', *Washington Post* (16 May 2017), www.washingtonpost.com.

8 Paul Colford, '"Illegal Immigrant" No More', *Associated Press* (2 April 2013), https://blog.ap.org; Rukhshona Nazhmidinova, 'User-generated Racism: Russia's Media and Migrants', European Journalism Observatory (20 November 2013), https://en.ejo.ch.

9 Herbert Klein, *The Atlantic Slave Trade* (Cambridge, 2010).

10 John Fuller, *The Interrupted Journey* (Berkeley, ca, 1966), which was filmed as *The ufo Incident* in 1975, starring Estelle Parsons and James Earl Jones. Two years later, Jones provided the voice of Darth Vader in the film *Star Wars*.

11 Budd Hopkins, *Missing Time* (New York, 1981); Whitley Strieber, *Communion: A True Story* (New York, 1987); David M. Jacobs, *Secret Life: Firsthand, Documented Accounts of ufo Abductions* (New York, 1992); John E. Mack, *Abduction: Human Encounters with Aliens* (New York, 1995).

12 Budd Hopkins, *Witnessed: The True Story of the Brooklyn Bridge ufo Abductions* (New York, 1996).

13 Susan Blackmore, 'Abduction by Aliens or Sleep Paralysis?', *Skeptical Inquirer*, xxii/3 (1998), available at https://skepticalinquirer.org.

14 Teresa Hunter, 'Do You Really Need Alien Insurance?', *The Telegraph* (28 June 2000), www.telegraph.co.uk.

15 H. G. Wells, *The War of the Worlds* (London, 1898).

16 Charlotte Edwardes and Catherine Milner, 'Egypt Demands Return of the Rosetta Stone', *The Telegraph* (20 July 2003), www.telegraph.co.uk.

17 Lancelot Hogben, *Science in Authority* (London, 1963), pp. 122–35.

18 The first in the 'Remembrance of Earth's Past' series, the award-winning *Three-Body Problem* (Chongqing, 2008) was translated by Ken Liu and published in English in 2014.

19 Karen Joy Fowler, 'The Great Silence by Ted Chiang', *Electric Literature* (12 October 2016), www.electricliterature.com. The last words of the iguaca parrot, of course, echo those of Alex, the grey parrot who worked closely with psychologist Irene Pepperberg for many years, and showed startling cross-species communicative ability (Benedict Carey, 'Alex, A Parrot Who Had A Way With Words, Dies', *New York Times* (10 September 2007), www.nytimes.com).

CONCLUSION: IMHUMANISM

1 A representative selection of the current crop of books we have in mind here includes Robin Dunbar, *The Human Story: A New History of Mankind's Evolution* (London, 2011); Yuval Noah Harari, *Sapiens: A Brief History of Humankind* (New York and London, 2014); Kenan Malik, *Man, Beast and Zombie: What Science Can and Cannot Tell Us About Human Nature* (New Brunswick, NJ, 2002); Jon Marks, *What It Means To Be 98% Chimpanzee* (Berkeley, CA, 2003). The genre, however, reaches back at least to the early twentieth century, and includes scholars such as Arthur Keith, Grafton Elliot Smith and H. J. Fleure as early practitioners.

2 Sarah Blaffer Hrdy, *Mothers and Others: The Evolutionary Origins of Mutual Understanding* (Cambridge, MA, 2009), pp. 1–32.

3 Carolyn D. Williams, 'Cogan, Thomas (1736–1818), Physician', *Oxford Dictionary of National Biography* (3 January 2008), available at www.oxforddnb.com, accessed 10 April 2019.

4 Samuel Glasse, *The Policy, Benevolence, and Charity of the Royal Humane Society* (London, 1793).

5 Donna Haraway, *Staying with the Trouble: Making Kin in the Chthulucene* (Durham, NC, 2016), p. 97.

6 Frantz Fanon, *The Wretched of the Earth* [1961], trans. Constance Farrington (London, 2001).

7 Nurit Bird-David, 'Size Matters! The Scalability of Modern Hunter-gatherer Animism', *Quaternary International*, CCCCLXIV, part A (10 January 2018), pp. 305–14.

8 Emma Alleyne and Bill Henry, 'The Psychology of Animal Cruelty: An Introduction to the Special Issue', *Psychology, Crime & Law*, XXIV/5 (2017), pp. 451–7.

9 Christopher D. Stone, 'Should Trees Have Standing – Toward Legal Rights for Natural Objects', *Southern California Law Review*, XLV (1972), pp. 450–501.

10 Alleyne and Henry, 'The Psychology of Animal Cruelty', pp. 496 and 456.

Select Bibliography

Aftandilian, Dave, 'Toward a Native American Theology of Animals:
   Creek and Cherokee Perspectives', *CrossCurrents*, LIX/2 (2011),
   pp. 191–207
Arendt, Hannah, *The Human Condition*, 2nd edn (Chicago, IL, 1998)
Battaglia, Debbora, ed., *E. T. Culture: Anthropology in Outerspaces*
   (Durham, NC, 2005)
Beard, Mary, *Women and Power: A Manifesto* (London, 2017)
Bradshaw, John, *The Animals Among Us: The New Science of
   Anthrozoology* (Harmondsworth, 2017)
Devlin, Kate, *Turned On: Science, Sex and Robots* (London, 2018)
Dupré, John, *Humans and Other Animals* (Oxford, 2006)
Fine, Cordelia, *Delusions of Gender: The Real Science Behind Sex
   Differences* (London, 2011)
Fudge, Erica, *Brutal Reasoning: Animals, Rationality and Humanity in
   Early Modern England* (Ithaca, NY, 2006)
Haraway, Donna, *When Species Meet* (Minneapolis, MN, 2007)
—, *Staying with the Trouble: Making Kin in the Chthulucene* (Durham,
   NC, 2016)
Harth, Erica, *Last Witnesses: Reflections on the Wartime Internment of
   Japanese Americans* (New York, 2001)
Hayles, N. Katherine, *How We Became Posthuman: Virtual Bodies in
   Cybernetics, Literature and Informatics* (Chicago, IL, 1999)
Hill, Donald, *Islamic Science and Engineering* (Edinburgh, 1993)
Hrdy, Sarah B., *Mothers and Others: The Evolutionary Origins of Mutual
   Understanding* (Cambridge, MA, 2011)
Humphrey, Louise, and Chris Stringer, *Our Human Story* (London, 2018)

Kapoor, Nisha, *Deport, Deprive, Extradite: 21st Century State Extremism* (London, 2018)

Keller, Vera, *Knowledge and the Public Interest, 1575–1725* (Cambridge, 2015)

Latour, Bruno, *Politics of Nature* (Cambridge, MA, 2004)

Long, Pamela O., *Artisan/Practitioners and the Rise of the New Sciences, 1400–1600* (Corvallis, OR, 2011)

MacCulloch, Diarmaid, *A History of Christianity: the First Three Thousand Years* (Harmondsworth, 2009)

McNeill, J. R., and William H. McNeill, *The Human Web: A Bird's-eye View of World History* (New York, 2003)

Marks, Jon, *What It Means to Be 98% Chimpanzee* (Berkeley, CA, 2003)

Meyer, Eric Daryl, *Inner Animalities: Theology and the End of the Human* (New York, 2018)

Miami Theory Collective and Georges Van Den Abbeele, eds, *Community at Loose Ends* (Minneapolis, MN, 1991)

Nagai, Kaori, et al., eds, *Cosmopolitan Animals* (London, 2015)

O'Gieblyn, Meghan, 'Ghost in the Cloud: Transhumanism's Simulation Theology', *n+1* (Spring 2017), www.nplusonemag.com

Oliver, Kelly, *Animal Lessons: How They Teach Us to Be Human* (New York, 2009)

Pankhurst, Helen, *Deeds Not Words: The Story of Women's Rights, Then and Now* (London, 2018)

Pomeroy, Sarah, *Goddesses, Whores, Wives and Slaves: Women in Classical Antiquity* (London, 1994)

Richardson, Sarah, *Sex Itself: The Search for Male and Female in the Human Genome* (Chicago, IL, 2013)

Rieder, John, *Colonialism and the Emergence of Science Fiction* (Middletown, CT, 2008)

Rooney, Caroline, *Decolonising Gender: Literature and a Poetics of the Real* (London, 2007)

Rutherford, Adam, *The Book of Humans: The Story of How We Became Us* (London, 2018)

Schaffer, Simon, *Mechanical Marvels: Clockwork Dreams*, BBC (2014)

—, *Mechanical Monsters*, BBC (2018)

Schnabel, Jim, *Dark White: Aliens, Abductions and the UFO Obsession* (London, 1994)

Shepard, Paul, *The Others: How Animals Made Us Human* (Washington, DC, 1996)

Sissons, Jeffrey, *First Peoples: Indigenous Cultures and their Futures* (London, 2005)

Smith, Pamela H., *The Body of the Artisan: Art and Experience in the Scientific Revolution* (Chicago, IL, 2004)

Stone, Christopher D., *Should Trees Have Standing? Law, Morality, and the Environment* (Oxford, 2010)

Stringer, Chris, *Lone Survivors: How We Came to Be The Only Humans on Earth* (London, 2012)

Tattersall, Ian, *The Last Neanderthal: The Rise, Success and Mysterious Extinction of Our Closest Human Relatives* (New York, 1995)

Torpey, John, *The Invention of the Passport: Surveillance, Citizenship and the State* (Cambridge, 2000)

Tresch, John, *The Romantic Machine: Utopian Science and Technology after Napoleon* (Chicago, IL, 2012)

Trinkaus, Eric, and Pat Shipman, *The Neandertals: Changing the Image of Mankind* (London, 1993)

Vint, Sherryl, *Animal Alterity: Science Fiction and the Question of the Animal* (Liverpool, 2010)

Voskuhl, Adelheid, *Androids in the Enlightenment: Mechanics, Artisans, and Cultures of the Self* (Chicago, IL, 2013)

Wells, H. G., *The Outline of History* (London, 1920)

Williams, Rowan, *Being Human: Bodies, Minds, Persons* (London, 2018)

Acknowledgements

With grateful thanks to Daniel Belteki and Tom Ritchie who conducted picture research for this book, and to participants in the Wunderkammer reading group at the Centre for the History of the Sciences, University of Kent, for the eclectic and knowledgeable conversations connected to the themes of this book. Amanda would like to thank colleagues at the University of York for their tolerant and helpful responses to (sometimes obscure) questions.

Photo Acknowledgements

120 (CC BY-SA 3.0): p. 46; Alamy: pp. 19 (Neil Setchfield), 56, 57, 104 (Chronicle), 106 (Mauritius Images GmbH), 131 (Godong), 139 (Mirelle Vautier), 152 (Erin Paul Donovan); Dr Mike Baxter (CC BY-SA 2.0): p. 53; Bodleian Libraries, University of Oxford: pp. 167, 176; Bridgeman Images: pp. 20 (Look and Learn /Illustrated Papers Collection), 26 (© British Library Board. All Rights Reserved); © The Trustees of the British Museum, London: p. 125; Brödbaron (CC BY-SA 4.0): p. 187; Czartoryski Museum and Library, Krakow: p. 34; Didier Descouens (CC BY-SA 4.0): p. 48; Detroit Institute of Arts: p. 147; Freud Museum, London: p. 41; Gallery Oldham: p. 134; Matthieu Gafsou: p. 142; Gemäldegalerie, Berlin: p. 37; Getty Images: pp. 83 (*Daily Herald* /SSPL), 90, 93 (SSPL); Glasgow University Library: p. 28; Herzogliches Museum, Gotha: p. 38; Larry Lamsa: p. 177; © 2019 Les Enluminures: p. 89; Library of Congress, Washington, DC: pp. 98, 151; Manalahmadkhan: p. 17; Matthias-Kabel (CC BY-SA 2.5): p. 10; Mariano (CC BY-SA 3.0): p. 12; MesserWoland (CC BY-SA 2.5): p. 155; The Metropolitan Museum, New York: pp. 24, 73, 75, 79, 126, 128, 138, 184, 185; Museum Boijmans Van Beuningen, Rotterdam: p. 120; Douglas Muth: p. 42; National Maritime Museum, Greenwich: p. 124; NASA: pp. 107, 161, 162; Newnham College, University of Cambridge: p. 58; National Gallery of Victoria, Melbourne: p. 145; National Museum of Fine Arts, Stockholm: p. 29 (Cecilia Heisser); National Oceanic and Atmospheric Administration (NOAA): p. 14 (Robert Pittman); National Portrait Gallery of Sweden: p. 181; NHM Images: p. 6; Arne Nordmann (CC BY-SA 3.0): p. 164; Palentine Gallery, Florence: p. 146; Parentesis99 (CC BY-SA 4.0): p. 143; © The Board of Trustees of the Science Museum, London: p. 70; Thilo Parg (CC BY-SA

Index

Page numbers in *italics* refer to illustrations